CONSCIOUS
LEADERSHIP

CONSCIOUS LEADERSHIP

And The Power of Energetic Fields

REBECCA WATSON

authorHOUSE®

AuthorHouse™ UK
1663 Liberty Drive
Bloomington, IN 47403 USA
www.authorhouse.co.uk
Phone: 0800.197.4150

Published by AuthorHouse 02/04/2015

ISBN: 978-1-5049-3614-9 (sc)
ISBN: 978-1-5049-3613-2 (e)

CONTENTS

What is The Big Picture?

Why You Should Read this Book

How I came to write this book

I have studied the question "What makes a person a great Leader?" for over 10 years. In that time, I have coached hundreds of leaders from private and public organisations, from entrepreneurs to artists. I have experimented with various different coaching techniques – some worked well, some didn't work at all! I have read many books across a multitude of disciplines too, all in the pursuit of "What makes a person a great leader?"

On this journey, I have also developed myself. I started off with all my fears about giving up a career in law to become a Leadership Coach. I worked on my own unconscious beliefs, experienced therapy, yoga and meditation. I travelled to explore other cultures and simply spoke to lots of people about their experience of leaders and what they thought made a good leader. For some reason I was drawn towards this path, and it has brought me challenge, immense joy and life-long friendships.

This book bridges two worlds. The world of traditional business (revenue, products, structure, and processes that can be measured) and the unseen world (thoughts, emotional responses, and energetic fields) that has a real effect on how successful a leader will be, but is unseen and cannot easily be measured. The unseen world is one that quantum physics has understood from a scientific perspective and consciously evolved people like the Dalai Lama have understood from a spiritual perspective.

I believe that my own purpose is to support leaders to raise their levels of conscious.

In short, I followed my intuition with my work and it has led me to understanding one of the *great secrets of leadership*. I aim to share that secret with you in this book.

Why you need to read this book

There are so many books on leadership, aiming to teach you how to improve – so why read this one?

In the past, we have misunderstood what makes someone a great leader. We have thought that it is about WHAT YOU DO. This is the focus of many books on leadership, but they are missing the core differentiator.

In this book, I explain the SECRET that most of the world does not seem to know yet.

It is the single differentiating factor between poor/average leaders and great leaders.

Once you know this SECRET, you will start to THINK, FEEL and BEHAVE differently as a Leader. You will become a more CONSCIOUS LEADER, and therefore, be able to work in a completely different way to create the results you want – for yourself, for your team and for your organisation.

What will I gain once I'm a Conscious Leader?

- You will have less anxiety/frustration at work
- You will be able to turn around those relationships that currently make you annoyed/upset/uncomfortable (including personal relationships)
- You will be more energy efficient, so leaving work less tired and able to have more energy for yourself/your family outside of work
- You will have tapped into a higher purpose for your work and the contribution your organisation makes to society, so you will see your career in a new light
- You will be able to tap into your creativity and be more innovative at work
- You will be able to get to the heart of a problem so long as that problem involves people because you will have a way of discovering how the problem has been created in the first place
- YOU WILL BE A GREAT LEADER AND CONTINUE TO DEVELOP ON THIS PATH FOR THE REST OF YOUR CAREER

What will my TEAM gain once I'm a Conscious Leader?

- Your team will be more aware of their purpose, their value and their contribution, and therefore, their work will feel more meaningful to them.
- Your team will become more productive because they will be absolutely clear on their direction and then have you to support them in the most effective way as a leader.
- You will be able to consciously shift groups of people who have become tired/frustrated/detached from difficult projects by refocusing their minds and energy
- You will know how to create a high performing culture within your organisation and will automatically create a higher performing culture within the entire section of the organisation you lead.

What will my ORGANISATION gain once I'm a Conscious Leader?

- If you are the CEO or responsible for attracting investors, you will know how to create a buzz in the market around your organisation and attract investors automatically.
- If you are the CEO or responsible or attracting customers/clients, you will know how to pitch your organisation and manage your customers/clients in such a way that you automatically attract more.
- Once your organisation has the benefit of Conscious Leaders, it will automatically attract the best talent in the market because everyone wants to work for an organisation that has a high performing culture with happy, empowered employees.

CHAPTER 1

What Are Levels of Consciousness?

Introduction

In this Chapter I will do the following:

- Explain what Consciousness is and why it is the first necessary step toward Great Leadership.
- Set out the things that Conscious Leaders know and do, so that you can compare where you are currently with where you will be when you have read this book.
- Introduce the concept of Levels of Consciousness, what this means and what criteria is used to determine your level of consciousness.
- Show how it is not so much WHAT YOU DO as a leader but WHO YOU ARE (or at what level of consciousness you are operating from) that determines your skill and results as a leader.

What is Consciousness?

Consciousness is simply being aware.

If you are conscious of something, you are now aware of it. You may not have been aware of it 10 minutes ago, but now you are. A fire alarm allows us to become consciously aware that we may be in in danger. Before the alarm went off, we may not have had any other way of knowing that there was a fire in the room below.

An easy way to show different levels of consciousness is to compare children of different ages. As we grow from small children to teenagers, we shift our view of the world, or ourselves, and we start to control our emotional responses to our environment.

When we were children, we had a worldview that was much smaller than the view we hold now. We were naïve, inexperienced and unable to understand that other people held different views from us. We used childish tactics to try to get what we wanted and were less able to compromise or put others first. We were leading our lives from a child-like "operating system" – a child's level of consciousness.

As adults, we have developed a more sophisticated operating system – an adult level of consciousness. As we continue to develop throughout our adult lives we can also move into higher, or more developed levels of adult consciousness. It is the different levels of operating systems that I call "levels of consciousness."

In all of my experience working with different leaders and researching the question "What makes a good Leader?" I have come to the conclusion that it is the level of consciousness that the leader is operating from in any given moment that makes the difference. Leaders who have developed their mindsets to a high level of consciousness will automatically be far better leaders than those who have not. This is what I set out to explain in this book.

We can only operate from the highest level of consciousness that we have experienced. We cannot operate from a level of consciousness that we have not yet experienced. However, under stress, we may regress momentarily and operate from a younger (and lower) level of consciousness.

The purpose of this book is to help you as leaders raise your level of consciousness. This means taking you, my reader, on a thought journey – a sequence of understandings, where you need to understand the first concept in order to understand the second concept and so on. This is how I have laid out this book, so to get the most out of this book, you should read each chapter in order.

To even begin to help people raise their levels of consciousness, I need to help them become consciously aware. It is like asking someone to give up their current day job and become a Formula One car mechanic. Firstly, they need to be aware that these cars exist and fully understand what they are! Secondly they need to understand how the engines work. Thirdly, they use this knowledge to improve the engine's efficiency and level of performance. Throughout, I need to keep persuading them that putting in the effort to learn to be a Formula One car mechanic is going to bring them greater benefits than staying in their day job. I need to motivate them to put in the effort.

So with leadership development, firstly, you need to be aware that you have a level of consciousness and fully understand what it is! Secondly, you need to understand how you work. Thirdly, you can use this knowledge to fine tune yourself as a Leader to gain efficiency and higher performance. Throughout this book, I also attempt to give you explanations of the benefits of putting in the effort to raise your level of consciousness as a leader. The ramifications are so vast that I have had to dedicate Chapters 8-14 to the benefits for yourself, your team, your organization and your society!

Why is becoming conscious important?

In order to develop as a leader, you need to first become as conscious as you can. This is just self-awareness. If I am aware of myself, I am consciously aware of the thoughts that I am having and the feelings I am having in my body. The thoughts that you have in your mind have a direct effect on the emotions you feel in your body, including any body tension and internal chemical reactions like releasing adrenalin. I explain this more fully in Chapter 4.

As a leader, you have a huge influence on the people around you, how those people feel, what they then do, and therefore, the overall state that the organisation is working in. You can therefore have either a positive or negative effect on these people and the output of your organisation. This also applies to your family and any social occasions you experience. We all know that if we are in a bad mood, then our family or friends will find it hard not to be affected by this. Our mood affects the mood of others and potentially our entire social experience! Yes, we've all been there as either the culprit or the observer of this social phenomena.

Most leaders are operating from an unconscious automatic self. They are not consciously aware of their own thoughts and how these thoughts affect their own emotional states and the fact that they bring this emotional state into the workplace!

They are only aware that of end results: an exhausted body; an unhappy PA; an under-performing team that doesn't take ownership; the common complaint "if I don't do it myself then nothing gets done"; and the feeling that they are dragging people through mud!

Your own thoughts, and therefore the emotional state that your body is in, will affect everyone around you. The role of leader doesn't always mean "Good Leader," but it always means "Powerful Influencer." Do you want to use this power for good or bad effect?

Being a Conscious Leader, in this book's definition, is also being consciously aware of the fact that you can develop yourself as an adult. You can shift your own level of consciousness from that of a low level (survival level) consciousness to a high levels. That is why I explain the models of Levels of Consciousness in Chapter 15. These models can be used as a guiding map for your own personal development as a leader throughout your career.

What do Conscious Leaders know and do?

1) They have an overview of the top three things that they need to be doing to be an effective leader. (Chapter 9)
2) They are aware of the feedback from their bodies – they are tapping into the Whole System to gain information and early warning signs. (Chapters 4 – 7)
3) They are aware of their own thoughts and how these affect their own energy and the outcomes in business that they are consciously seeking. (Chapter 10)
4) They can consciously manage their own emotional responses – remaining calm in crisis, energizing their teams when despondency strikes and ensuring that their own energy levels can cope with the high demands of the job. (Chapter 6)
5) They can consciously reprogram themselves in the moment, so consistently maintaining the best WAY OF BEING in any circumstance - like an eagle minutely readjusting its wings to hover in the thermals. (Chapter 7)
6) They understand how relationships REALLY work and consciously build strong and positive relationships all around them. (Chapter 5)
7) They know that energy is contagious and consciously use this to their advantage; they can create high performing cultures and a buzz in the market place. (Chapter 11)
8) They understand the Law of Attraction and use this to attract new customers/clients, investors and the top talent. (Chapter 11)

An in-depth explanation of the above is covered in the rest of this book.

What are levels of Consciousness?

There are many models of different levels of Consciousness and I have set out some of them in Chapter 15. They are attempts to show the different development stages of an individual's mindset. The theory is that as you experience life, you may develop your level of consciousness i.e., how you perceive the world, what you value, your level of self-awareness, and your ability to 'go with the flow'.

The components that make up your level of consciousness are:

1) Core beliefs: your beliefs about yourself, other people, your purpose, the world, how to get what you want, etc. I call these core operating beliefs and discuss this more fully in Chapter 7 on Reprogramming Our Operating Systems. In this Chapter, I set out some of the core beliefs that Great Leaders have so that you can "try these beliefs on" for yourself and see if they affect how you then lead.

2) Values: what you value and therefore strive to gain for yourself is different at each level of consciousness. This is explained in Chapter 15 and particularly in Richard Barrett's Model of Consciousness.

3) Self-awareness and responsibility: whether or not you are consciously aware of your own thoughts and how these are affecting your emotional state. If you are aware and take responsibility for your own thoughts and state (and therefore actions), then you can consciously chose to operate from a higher level of consciousness. This is the purpose of this book, to help you identify what level of consciousness you are in, what level you'd like to move to and give you the tools to do that. If you are unaware of how you are creating your own thoughts and emotional reaction to a situation, you may blame other people/things on for their experiences and not know that you have the power to change the situation and to chose how you react. You will not be able to consciously grow and develop, but will instead be continuously fighting the same

battle, or coming up against the same block in your career path.

4) Go with the flow: your ability to tap into your inner-self/true-self and be guided by this part of you is also a key differentiator of your level of consciousness. Barrett uses the term "soul" for this inner-self/true-self. In his model, he states that those operating from the lower levels of consciousness are guided by their ego, but those operating from the higher levels of consciousness are guided by their souls.

It is not WHAT YOU DO as a Leader but YOUR LEVEL OF CONSCIOUSNESS that makes the difference.

If we take the example of a highly consciously developed parent, they will be mature, wise, and able to manage their own emotional responses. They will understand that their child is not deliberately trying to be annoying, they just don't know any better. They will hold beliefs such as "It is my job to help my child learn in a compassionate way, so that my child learns in an environment which is full of LOVE and NO JUDGEMENTS."

In comparison, we can observe the parent who is not yet consciously developed and is still more like a child themselves, who is unable to manage their own emotional responses, so he/she shouts and screams at children, or even hits them out of rage and frustration. We all know that one parent is automatically going to be better than the other, not because of WHAT THEY DO but because of THEIR LEVEL OF CONSCIOUSNESS – because of how consciously developed they are.

As with the example of the different parents, it is the same with leaders. We have been teaching our leaders WHAT TO DO but we have not really understood that it is more important to help them develop THEIR LEVEL OF CONSCIOUSNESS. That what they think, say, do, decide and how they speak, solve problems, interact with others and run their teams/organisations will ALL come from THEIR LEVEL OF CONSCIOUSNESS.

But can I change who I am? Do I want to?

We also used to think that children's brains developed until adulthood and then we are sort of 'fixed' in our perception of the world and our personalities. However, studies in the field of neuroscience and behavioural science have demonstrated that adult brains continue to develop and change throughout our lives.

Example:

Susanne Cook-Grueter presented a model in 1994 with four levels of ego development. The first two stages describe ego development into adulthood. The second stage was described as "conventional" and she states that 90% of the general adult population function within the first two tiers of development.

> In contrast, the higher two tiers, the post conventional and the transcendent, describe rarer and more complex ways of how adults make sense of experience. The third tier is called post-formal or post-conventional because it goes beyond the modern, linear-scientific Western mindset and beyond the conventions of society by starting to question the unconsciously held beliefs, norms and assumptions about reality acquired during socialization and schooling.
>
> - Susanne R. Cook-Grueter, "Mature Ego Development: A Gateway to Ego Transcendence," *Journal of Adult Development,* Vol 7, No. 4.

So in order for leaders to move beyond the 90% population and into a higher level of consciousness, they need to start questioning their unconsciously held beliefs (about themselves, others and the world) that they have acquired during their upbringing.

Susanne states that 9% of the population is in the third stage where they are not fixed in their world view based on their own socialization and 1% of the population have reached what she calls the "ego-transcendent" stage of consciousness.

Why would you want to join the Top 10%?

Once you to move to the third and forth tier in Susanne R. Cook-Grueter's model, you are a Conscious Leader and will gain all the benefits for yourself personally as well as your team and your organisation set out in the Introduction to this book and explained in more detail in Chapters 8-14.

I haven't even touched on the world influence you could bring if your path is as powerful as that of Mahatma Ghandi or Nelson Mandela! You may not fully know yet what your purpose in life is. You may not have reached that level of consciousness (see Richard Barrett's Model for more information on this in Chapter 15).

Will this change my personality and whole life?

This book is not aimed at changing anyone's personality. It is written to help you become consciously aware of your held beliefs, norms, and assumptions about reality so that you can move into the third tier of Susanne R. Cook-Grueter's model. Your fundamental personality and what you love in life won't change, but you will mature. You will grow into the best version of yourself as a leader. This can only bring more balance and harmony to your life and those around you.

Chapter Summary

- You now know what consciousness is and why it is the first necessary step toward great leadership.
- You have a template for what Conscious Leaders know and do, so that you can begin to compare where you are currently with where you will be when you have read this book.
- You know what is meant by "Levels of Consciousness" and what criteria are used to determine your level of consciousness.

- It is not so much WHAT YOU DO as a leader but HOW YOU ARE BEING that determines your success.
- In the next chapter, I'll help you identify what type of leadership you are currently operating from and some of the ways you can shift to the next level.

CHAPTER 2

What Level Am I As a Leader? How To Fast Track Through the Stages.

Introduction

In this Chapter I will:
- Set out my basic three-stage model of different levels of leadership so you can identify with the stage/stages you are currently in.
- Disclose the average level of leadership in our current culture. If you are reading this book, I am guessing that you are already at a higher level than your average leader!
- Discuss what can happen if a leader raises their level of consciousness within their organization – a preview of what may happen for you. Please keep reading. J
- Set out how to fast track your leadership development.

What level am I as a leader?

So far, I have discussed lots of concepts, but how does this actually affect you as a leader? What is the different experience of a leader operating from one level of consciousness to a leader operating from a higher level of consciousness? In Chapter 15, there are various models of human consciousness, which briefly explain the experience and what you will value at each level.

Through my role as a Leadership Coach, I have developed my own basic model to help clients identify at what level they are as leaders and to show them the next level.

I have called the three stages Mechanical Leadership, Strategic Leadership, and Inspirational Leadership, and each stage represents a higher level of consciousness within the leader.

Stage 1 – Mechanical Leadership

This phase is identifiable by the leader thinking mostly about what he/she must do. They often have "to do" lists that they are focusing on getting through during the day. They often spend a huge amount of time responding to emails and generally operating in a reactive way to their environment. They are interrupted by others. They do not feel in control of their time and can end up in meeting after meeting throughout the day. They may often start the 'real' work at 5 p.m. when the meetings are over.

- Their mantra is "There's not enough time" or "I need better staff" or both.

- They have a first-position mindset — i.e., from their own position, looking out through their own eyes, they ask "What do I need to do?"

- Their focus is mostly "small picture" – i.e., only seeing what they are doing during the day. They focus on directly producing results alongside the rest of the individuals in their team.

- They have low Emotional Intelligence Quotas (Daniel Goleman) – i.e., they are not very aware of their own bodies and how they feel throughout the day, so can have angry outbursts, or an accumulation of held tension in the body leading to headaches, neck, shoulder ache, stomach problems, etc.

- They have low Social Intelligence Quotas (Daniel Goleman) – i.e., they are unaware of the emotional states of those around them and do not know how to speak tactfully. They are often surprised if people become upset or angry with them.

Those stuck in Mechanical Leadership may not be consciously aware of the difference between strategic and non-strategic activities on their 'to do' list. Those ready to move to the next stage of Leadership Development will know that they are caught doing mostly non-strategic activities and have a desire to free up more time in order to think strategically.

Stage 2 – Strategic Leadership

A leader that is developed to this level is focused on the group/team and what "we" need to achieve. They have time to think strategically as well as time to do their own activities. The purpose of their role has shifted from "producing" to "coaching/mentoring/leading the team to produce."

- Their mantra is "What do we need to achieve?" "Where are we going?" "How can I help my team?"

- They have a group mindset – i.e., focused on how the team members are interacting with each other to achieve results.

- They have the ability to build good relationships with most of their team. However, the team probably knows who they struggle to connect with and who frustrates them.

- Their focus is the "bigger picture" – i.e., on what the team has to produce and how they can best work together to achieve this. Their activities include delegating work, coaching and mentoring staff, managing team meetings effectively to keep motivation high as well as keeping the team focused on moving towards team goals.

- They are more aware of their own body, the emotional states they are in and how this affects others. They therefore develop greater emotional intelligence for those they work with.

- They feel in control to a certain extent, although the wider organisation may interrupt the work their team is doing.

Stage 3 – Inspirational Leadership

This final stage of Leadership Development is one where the leader has a sense of purpose and meaning for their role within the organisation and their life as a whole. They have a sense of corporate and individual responsibility because they see that everything is connected and that each individual has a responsibility to the whole. They have a way of being that others find attractive and people will naturally follow these leaders even if they are not in a senior leadership role. They are powerful influencers, well liked, but perhaps feared by leaders that are not so highly developed. They are inspirational to others who will unconsciously start to copy the way these leaders do things. In doing so, these leaders can improve the entire culture of the area of the organisation that they lead.

- Their mantra is "Who am I? Am I walking my talk? What is my purpose?" and "Am I still energized by what I'm doing? Am I on my right path in life?"

- They have a whole system mindset — i.e., their focus covers not just coaching/mentoring their own team, but also smoothing the way for their team through influencing others within the organisation and potentially seeing how a radical change across a wider area could improve the company as a whole.

- They also have a positive mindset — i.e., their general views of the world, other people and themselves are positive. They have compassion for people and see their potential, and they believe their team/company will succeed.

- They are proactive in closely monitoring those that are not maintaining their standard and are compassionate with those that they feel need to leave the organisation. They will have a successful track record of performance management as well as a reputation for transparency.

- They have a "big picture" view because they see the entire system and how it is connected. They see themselves, their team, how their team interacts with other teams, the company, how the company is acting in the world and its effects.

- These leaders are consciously aware, meaning that they understand that our thoughts create reality and are very aware of their own thoughts. They understand that emotions are contagious, so they are well practiced in bringing themselves back to a calm state. They view their bodies as feedback systems, so also hear the message their body is signaling to them and act on this. This helps them make extremely good decisions. They understand the universal laws of attraction and use this to attract new business/people/opportunities.

- They feel passionate about change for the greater good. They feel energized by results that they can achieve, and they are empowered to make a difference. Because they have a positive mindset, they can face huge challenges and stay centered and calm throughout.

- They attract people who want to work for them and with them. When these leaders are in a client-facing role, they attract clients automatically rather than having to work to gain new clients. If these leaders are entrepreneurs or CEOs, they will lead the company to success. The smaller the company, the quicker the shift, but eventually all CEOs in this stage of leadership development create highly successful organisations.

What is the norm?

In over 10 years, I have worked with leaders across all sorts of organisations including military leaders, school Headmistresses, entrepreneurs, actresses as well as an array of bankers, lawyers, doctors, CEOs, HR, IT technicians, sales and marketing Directors, CFOs and MDs.

If you identify yourself as stuck in Stage 1 as a Mechanical Leader, it may be impossible for you to imagine being an Inspirational Leader in Stage 3. Even the description may be hard to comprehend. You may be saying to yourself "Stage 3 is just a dream world; it's not possible" or "The commercial world doesn't need Inspirational Leaders; those are just do-gooders or world peacemakers."

Many leaders that I have worked with feel that they are straddling Mechanical Leadership and Strategic Leadership. My work with them initially helps them move entirely to Stage 2, Strategic Leadership, and this can be very difficult if they are in an organisation where nearly all the leaders are Mechanical Leaders. If this is the case for you (and it is commonly the case in our current society), then as you shift to Strategic Leadership, you will start to become counter-cultural. You will start to operate from a higher level of consciousness. I discuss what can happen in this case below. Knowing this gives my clients an advantage in being able to also deal with the ramifications of them developing within their organisation.

What happens if I am at a different level of consciousness?

Leaders will lead with the mindset and way of being that is characterized by the level of consciousness that they have attained. This will also have a knock on effect on the organisations or societies that they lead because the group that is led will be inhibited from developing beyond the level of consciousness of its leader(s).

As you develop as a leader, you will see very clearly how to change the way your organisation is operating in order to gain much higher results and a higher performing culture. This can often cause frustration as others are slow to understand your perspective. For that reason, being compassionate, humble, and knowing how to communicate your ideas is key. If you can get enough people on board with your new ideas, you will be able to work together to transform your organisation (or department or team, depending on how senior you are in the hierarchy). Courage is a key trait for leaders who want to speak their truth as they see it and who are actively bucking the trend. However, huge rewards and personal satisfaction can ensue.

Sometimes, those who are operating from a higher level of consciousness will often seek the freedom of thought, speech, and action that may not be permissible within their organisation or society.

Eventually, they may have no alternative but to leave their organisation and find a leadership role within another organisation that is already operating from this higher level of consciousness.

This is most common with the junior leaders that I coach, who are not listened to and feel so frustrated that they seek a more enlightened organisation in which to bring their full potential into the world.

Losing talent is one of the key problems with organisations that have leaders at the top that are operating at a lower level of consciousness than the more junior leaders.

Example:

Case study

I once worked with a senior leader of a global investment bank who felt that they were being bullied by their boss and his colleagues. When my client understood that they were operating as a Strategic Leader (and sometimes as an Inspirational Leader) in an environment where everyone else unconsciously operated from Mechanical Leadership, they realized that the core problem was not personal!

The other leaders that surrounded my client often displayed bursts of anger and a sense of panic. Because of their inefficient way of operating they also had to work extremely long hours. This was interpreted as (a) normal behavior and (b) proof that the leader really cared about their situation. By the same token, it meant that my client was viewed as someone who was (a) not normal, (b) not one of us and (c) a leader who didn't really care about their situation.

My work with this leader helped them realize that there was nothing "wrong" with them and that they were only counter cultural. My work also included helping my client see that there was also nothing "wrong" with the other leaders in the organisation – that they were just unconsciously operating from a different level of consciousness and were not deliberately bullying my client, but were struggling within themselves to accept my client's behaviours.

Eventually, my client chose to leave the organisation and become a leader in a different organisation where the culture was one created by leaders operating at the same (or higher) level of consciousness as them.

How do I fast track through the stages?

I believe it is possible to fast track through these stages, but this requires an immersion of the mind and body in pursuit of transformation. It is hard to gain through traditional based learning (learning through understanding the theory) and requires experiential learning (learning through applying the theory and experiencing results through the body as well as the mind). Below are some ideas of how to fast track your development:

- Use this book.
In this book, I aim to explain why Leaders who operate from a higher level of consciousness are more successful. I also set out some exercises along the way that you can do to actually begin to shift your level of consciousness straight away.

- Use a highly conscious coach.
To shift your level of consciousness (i.e., your mindset and how you then operate in the world) without the aid of an experienced third party is very hard. We are trying to use the same brain that got us this far, to get us to the next stage, and this, by definition, has inherent problems!

The use of a coach who is highly conscious and has experience as a guide for Leaders moving to greater levels of consciousness is one option. At some level, any use of **an independent third party** – who will listen without judgment and reflect back to you, the thoughts that you are running, as opposed to giving you their opinion on what you should do –
will help. This is unlikely to be family members, friends, or work colleagues because to varying levels you are in an inter-dependent relationship with all of these people.

- Wait for life to happen!
Often people fast track to higher levels of consciousness due to an intense personal crisis or near death experience. It does not have

to be this dramatic if learning can happen in a safe and conscious environment. However, some leaders will simply become highly conscious due to their life experiences, without having to actively work on it with a coach or other independent third party.

You may know people who seem centered, wise and compassionate while others are judgmental – maybe mature beyond their age. These leaders may have been lucky enough to have been raised by enlightened people, or had the support of someone to overcome a personal crisis – e.g., challenging childhood experiences, unexpected loss of loved ones, the survival of a natural disaster, or an emotional or physical breakdown.

- Leave your comfort zone

For the last five years, I have run a leadership retreat in Spain – I invited some of my advanced clients to step out of their comfort zone (literally) and into an environment that is peaceful, close to nature, with long views over the sea and mountains, all to help the body and mind relax.

The idea was to create an environment (both physical as well as emotional) that was conducive to my clients being able to shift rapidly – i.e., have those 'light bulb moments' that can't be forced.

- Calm the mind.

It seems to me that we are most likely to have these shifts in moments of relaxation, when the mind is open, rather than fixed on the "to do" list! To help bring my clients to this state was often much more difficult when doing a 1-2 hour coaching session in their offices.

You may say, "Well, that's all well and good, but right now I can't work with a coach" or "I don't want to wait to attend some annual leadership retreat in Spain!" In which case, my advice right now, would be to decide to do things that will help calm the mind in your every day life. Yoga, Tai Chi, Meditation, or simply walking on your own in nature could be some of the ways you can start this work immediately.

Chapter Summary

By reading this chapter, you should be able to now:

- Identify which stage/stages you are currently experiencing in my three stage Leadership Model.
- Feel quite pleased with yourself for either being above average level of leadership in our current culture – or at least excited about the fact that you hold the key to shift in your hands right now!
- Be aware of some of the consequences of reading this book and raising your level of consciousness (more on this in Chapters 8 - 14).
- Have some ideas of what you can do right now to start fast tracking your development.

In Chapter 3, I will discuss how we all want the same core traits in our leaders and what those traits are.

CHAPTER 3

What Traits Do We Want In Our Leaders?

Introduction

In this Chapter, I will:
- Ask "what are the core leadership traits that we admire and are likely to willingly follow?"
- Explain how humans all identify with certain core traits, whatever era they lived in and whatever culture they come from.
- Discuss each core trait – although this list is not exhaustive.

What traits do we want In our Leaders?

Many changes are happening across the globe right now that have contributed to our society asking the key question: "What do we want our Leaders to DO and NOT DO?" I go into more details in Chapter 16 as to why I think this question is now being raised.

Because we can't have a "one size fits all" answer to the question, we start to discuss HOW they should behave generally – e.g., ethical leadership is currently the buzz topic.

Ethical leadership on its own doesn't mean anything. You as a leader need to know what acting ethically looks like. You need to identify with the traits of ethical leaders and consciously operate from these same personality traits in order to be called ethical.

The same principal applies to you if want to be a great leader. You need to identify the personality traits that great leaders have had over time and connect to the same personality traits inside of you.

You have an inbuilt 'great leader detector.'

This could start to get complex. However, the lucky thing is that I believe deep down, all of us instinctively know what great leadership traits are. We have inbuilt "Great Leader" detectors.

We know when we have worked with a great leader because we know how it made us feel. The leader was operating from certain personality traits like courage and honesty and being around them helped us connect to our own courage and honesty and this felt good. Just by being around them, we were automatically operating as our best selves.

We also know when we have worked with a leader who is not operating from these "Great Leader" traits and who may be operating out of insecurity and blame and how that made us feel.

Ordinary people across the ages and across all cultures, have known deep down that the traits of great leaders are those such as honesty, courage, acting for the greater good, ability to rise above the fears, political maneuvering of those they lead, etc.

So how is this possible?

I believe that we all have the capability to have all personality traits. We just tend to act from a few of them and that is how we get "coded" with a personality type. I go into more detail on this in Chapter 7. So I believe that we can all connect to our courage, our honesty and our ability to see what is best for the greater good and not just for ourselves.

When we see another human acting from these traits, it allows us to connect with our own ability to do this (almost like reminding us that we can step up too and all be great leaders). This reminder can either make us feel great because we are motivated to join the Leader and connect to our own courage/honesty *or* it makes us feel guilty/jealous/negative in some way because we feel that we can't connect to these traits in ourselves, but here is someone right in front of us who can. In this case, we may ridicule them, or put them down to our friends and "Who do they think they are?" statements might be uttered.

In fact the great leader who is calling to the rest of his or her people to follow them, is really saying "Look what traits I can connect with and look at who I can be – you can do exactly the same!' They are not saying "Look how much better I am than you." They are trying to call you to join them. Be the same as them, because deep down they hold a belief that if encouraged and supported enough, everyone can connect to these same traits. This is the true work of the inspirational Leader.

That is how anyone and everyone can be a good leader. The organisational or societal role, which is labeled "Leader," does not mean that the person who currently has that role is a good leader; it just means that they are playing this role to the best of their ability.

There are true leaders amongst the whole population who are demonstrating great leadership all around us. They may not be labeled "leader," but they are calling out to others to join them, to walk with them towards the vision/goal that this true leader is inspired to achieve. You may be one of these leaders or know people like this. You are the ones who are trying to change the status quo in some way and (in your mind) trying to change it for the better for everyone, not just for yourselves. You are not just trying to remain in power or gain power for yourself.

Are you the hero of your own life story?

Joseph Campbell studied many different myths and stories of heroes across cultures and also across time. His research led him to understand that from ancient Greek mythology to modern day fairy tales, humans have used symbolism to describe one classic person (our hero/heroine) and one classic journey (the journey to develop our own psyche/level of consciousness).

In his book *The Hero With A Thousand Faces,* he tells us that "The standard path of the mythological adventure of the hero is a magnification of the formula represented in the rites of passage." He compares the mythological interpretations with words of spiritual leaders such as Moses, Jesus, Mohammed, Lao-tse, and the Old Man of Australian tribes. He shows how we are all on this same developmental journey and we have all got the capability to display these hero/Leadership traits. That is why we identify with the classic storyline, deep down, we see ourselves as the hero and want to be as good as them.

The storyline and lead character in the film *Star Wars* created by George Lucas is a perfect example of this. Cinderella and Harry Potter are also stories that follow the classic "hero journey" described by Joseph Campbell. The lead character (our hero, with whom we identify) begins the story in an unfortunate situation (e.g., Cinderella and Harry Potter are both orphans living in a family environment that is harsh for them). Then something happens, or someone comes to them, in order to help them move from this situation. They meet someone "special" who supports them to move forward.

The story unfolds with the lead character (our hero, with whom we identify) taking risks to reach an end goal. They also grow and develop as people during the story. If we were to look back on how they were at the start of the story to how they are at the end, we see a marked difference, not just in circumstances, but in their life experiences, and therefore their confidence in themselves and their abilities to overcome challenge.

They are stories of personal development of the hero, featuring mythical characters that help the hero transform during his personal journey.

This, Joseph Campbell states, is everyone's journey of personal development. It is also why people who have come further on this personal development journey than others, make better Leaders. They already have enough experiences in life to know who they are and what they can do. They have already had someone call to them, to step up and connect to their great Leader traits such as courage and honesty. They have already acted from these traits and experienced the ramifications (the reactions of people around them, some positive, some negative). They are already operating from a certain level of consciousness as a human being.

Core leadership traits

Below are some of the core leadership traits. This is obviously not an exhaustive list, but when I'm working with leaders, these are the most common traits with which I am helping my clients connect with in order to overcome a challenge or move towards their vision/goals. These traits seem to be the ones that haven't changed over time and across cultures. They are at least some of the base human traits of great leadership.

Self awareness

> Know Thyself.
> - Plato, 428BC – 347BC

If you understand your own strengths and weaknesses as a leader, you have a much higher chance of outsourcing the activities that do not play to your strengths and remaining with the activities which you naturally find easy and are probably best at doing. I have yet to meet a leader who can do it all!

At a more profound level, leaders who are continuously learning about themselves, (what they really think and how this leads them to feel and what that then leads them to do or say) are most likely to develop to higher levels of consciousness. Many people avoid self analysis; however, those who do not have the chance to chose how to live their lives, rather than live a life of repeated unconscious behaviours.

For all the experience I have working with leaders, the most humbling is the knowledge that every person who choses to work with me, has the courage and desire to become more self-aware.

Centered, clear thinking

> If you can keep your head when all about you
> Are losing theirs and blaming it on you;
> If you can trust yourself when all men doubt you,
> But make allowance for their doubting too.
> - extract from Rudyard Kipling's poem *"If"*

The ability to stay calm and level-headed in a crisis allows leaders to make good decisions when faced with hugely challenging situations. Kipling's description also includes holding to your own truth, even when other people are doubting you. The line above describes the ability to have compassion for others who may not have your level of consciousness, rather than angrily judging and blaming them. This level of wisdom and compassion allows leaders to stay detached from the dramas that others are embroiled in around them.

There has been a recent resurgence in the UK of the strap line "Keep Calm and Carry On" which was created originally during the Second World War. The popularity of mugs, tea-towels, etc. displaying this brand and strap line has been so successful, because it is a message with which we identify. We aim to be that person and respect leaders who demonstrate this, too.

James Bond is a good example of a hero/leader who demonstrates his ability to stay calm and level-headed even when his life is at risk. On the other hand, the typical villains in the Ian Flemming's James Bond novels are characterized by the leaders found at level 3 consciousness in the Spiral Dynamics model – feudal, gang leaders with a need to control and prone to childish tantrums. I discuss this model in Chapter 15.

Choosing the right path – Ethical Leadership

Another trait that we wish to see demonstrated in our leaders is the ability to choose the "right" path, the path of moral high ground. This path will often lead to benefiting many, rather than just benefiting the leader. The theme of ethical leadership is not new. However, in modern times, there has been a resurgence of the importance of ethics in business.

Heesun Wee in an article for Bloomberg Business Week in 2002 stated:

> After the dust from the Enron collapse settles, one positive outcome may arise. CEOs, take note: The energy trader's demise provides an important lesson in the value - the necessity, really - of having a corporate conscience and a culture built around knowing the difference between right and wrong. It's tempting to brush aside business ethics as a nebulous, well-intentioned subject suitable for Business School 101 but of little practical value in the real world. Big mistake. Now we know the heavy toll that ignoring ethics can exact.

Ethical Leadership is now a hot topic. In the March 2012 edition of *Forbes*, an article on "The World's Most Ethical Companies" states: "The Ethisphere Institute, a New York City think tank, has just announced its sixth annual list of the World's Most Ethical Companies."

Alex Brigham, executive director of the Ethisphere Institute, has said, "Companies that are ethical tend to realize that doing the right thing is actually good for business - and they drive and encourage a culture that emphasizes that."

Leaders with a high level of consciousness will have the ability to hold many points of view. They will listen to the voice of "do whatever is necessary to make the most money right now" (the need for immediate gratification) as well as the voice of "we must look at the possible long term outcomes of our actions and ensure that there are no negative impacts on our employees and customers" (the need for long term sustainability) and find a higher path where both needs can be met. In Chinese philosophy, this is called "The Middle Way."

Note also that in their own lives, leaders who operate from this level of consciousness will also be able to make decisions for themselves that are a balance between what will bring them happiness in the current moment and what will bring them happiness in the long term.

Courage

Courage to do the 'right' thing despite the risk to themselves is one of the key themes of heroes. It is also one of the key traits the world needs right now in its business and political leaders.

We all seem to have an inbuilt sense of what is "right." This inbuilt sense is sometimes drowned out by our inner voice of fear – e.g., fear of failure, fear of the ramifications of speaking our truth, fear of being singled out, fear of not fitting in or being laughed at for an idea.

Steve Jobs stated:

> Your time is limited, so don't waste it living someone else's life. Don't be trapped by dogma - which is living with the results of other people's thinking. Don't let the noise of others' opinions drown out your own inner voice. And most important, have the courage to follow your heart and intuition.

We instinctively admire people who are able to do this. However, their courage serves to remind us that we could also be walking this courageous path, and this may lead us to feel uncomfortable mixing with them or resentful. We may give ourselves many reasons why it was possible for them to do it, but not for us.

One of the most common thought traps we run for ourselves is the fear of losing our job, not having enough money, and therefore, eventually not surviving if we listen to our heart and take a risk.

Many of my private career coaching clients feel that they cannot follow their dreams because they have financial commitments that must be met. One of the key exercises I ask them to complete is to work out how much money per month they actually need to live comfortably. I then ask them what monthly payments they can reduce/stop to move to this state – an obvious one is downsizing their home, or moving to a lower cost area to live. However, often it is simply our belief that we cannot earn as much money from doing what we love as we can from staying in our current jobs. Of course, there is likely to be a transition period where you may need to build a business from scratch and make key investments – but in the long run, if you are truly bringing to the world something of value, that you are passionate about, the income will support your new lifestyle.

I believe that courage is in all of us. For one person, the courage to take a new route to work is a big stretch. For another person, the courage to speak their truth in a board meeting might be their stretch. Each time we stretch ourselves, we are presented with a bigger potential stretch because we are now ready for it. When we don't take courage and act in the world as we know in our hearts of hearts we wish we could, we compromise a part of ourselves and this can lead to procrastination, discontent, boredom, frustration and, in some cases, physical or emotional issues.

The courage to be honest and transparent is something that organisations have traditionally struggled with. If you have the courage to compassionately do the right thing, then you will gain huge respect from those you lead. You will gain their trust, too.

Case study

I recently worked with a leader (let's call her Alison) who was struggling to come back to a place of calm with one of the Executive Team members (who I'll call James). James was displaying behaviors that led Alison to become increasingly frustrated with him. I asked about her fear: "What is the fear behind your anger?" She realized that her frustration was born out of a fear that James's behavior would jeopardize her organisation's success and therefore her own personal success in her career.

I then asked her to close her eyes and imagine that she had become James. I started speaking to her as if she was James, saying "Hi, James. Thanks for speaking to me today." "That's alright", she said, giggling at the absurdity of my exercise.

I said, "James, where do you live?" She replied,

"Where do you work James?" She replied, getting more serious about the exercise.

I asked, "James, what role do you play?" She started to speak as if she was James.

I then asked, "How are you feeling right now?" and her response was "overwhelmed." I asked, "Are you enjoying this job and working for Alison?"

She responded, still with her eyes closed, "No, I hate it. I know that I'm failing and I don't want to do this anymore."

"What is it you'd like to do instead?" I asked.

With her eyes still closed, intuitively Alison replied instantly, "I think the most important thing I could do is to raise my children."

She opened her eyes and stopped imagining she was James. "Wow" she said, "I guess I hadn't realized what it was like for him. I know he's said quite a few things about being happy for his wife to be the bread winner and how he thought that the most important job in the world is to help develop the next generation, but I didn't put two and two together until now. I must check this out with him."

"What is the most compassionate thing to do here?" I asked. In this case, she decided to have a more honest and compassionate conversation with James.

Sometimes letting people go to find their true path is compassionate and can be done in such a way that that person does not feel like a failure. They are just in the wrong job, wrong organisational culture or not following their true path.

Don't hide behind restructuring!

Your responsibility as a Conscious Leader is to make sure you have the right people on your team. Help those who aren't in the right roles move on, then do it openly and honestly. Don't just restructure which is what a lot of companies do, because this is not an honest process for making people who are not operating at the right level redundant. Everyone knows this, so they fear restructuring. A huge amount of energy is lost through destabilizing the work force.

If you have an honest and open conversation with someone about their performance and you question if they are in the right role, they may voluntarily leave (and thank you in years to come!). If not, then you can be honest about starting a performance management process and if the person still cannot, or does not, reach the required standard and leaves, you are sending a powerful message to the rest of the organisation about honesty, integrity and non-tolerance of low standards.

Faith

In order to "trust yourself when all men doubt you," you need to have faith in yourself. Faith is often connected to religion, but in this case, I am using the term in a broader sense. You may gain your faith from your religion, but if not, then it will come from your past experiences. If you have managed to do something that you initially didn't think you could do, then you have built a sense of faith in your ability. If you have stood up for what you think is right and been heard and respected, then you can gain a sense of faith in your beliefs about what is right and wrong.

If we had particularly bossy, critical or controlling parents, we may need to work a little harder on developing our own sense of faith.

A sense of personal faith can be built through daily practice. One of the basic exercises I suggest is to first connect to your true self by finding a place of peace and quiet (often many leaders do not prioritize time to do this) and listening to your real truth. Then, these quiet moments – just being honest with yourself about what you really think and how you really feel – can help build a sense of faith in yourself and help you make better decisions.

Leaders need to learn to connect to the part of them that is constant, calm and centered – the inner voice of reason. As a leader, you may have many times when you need to connect back to this place and ask, "Am I right? Are they right? What is my own truth?" Again and again, this inner voice of reason will respond and reassure, once you have built a good connection to it.

Nelson Mandela was a great example of a leader who had faith and total conviction in what he was trying to do. He was imprisoned for 27 years – 18 of those on Robben Island, off the coast of Cape Town. Mandela was completely isolated, forced to pound rocks as a form of work, and had little to eat, but even still, he had faith in his cause.

During this time, Gay McDougall was director of the Southern African Project of the Lawyers' Committee for Civil Rights Under Law, assisting in the defense of thousands of political prisoners in South Africa.

She said in an interview that Mandela knew he was serving a larger purpose in jail and didn't hold it against the guards: "That lack of personal animosity toward those in charge of his confinement was important to his survival."

How does this relate to leaders today, though?

In times of uncertainty, people will follow someone who is certain. It's a human trait to feel uncomfortable with uncertainty – often waiting for "the news" is worse than hearing that it's "bad news." At least once we are certain of something, we can start to adapt to it. So if you can listen to varied opinions, then bring yourself back to a calm place, connect to your inner voice of wisdom and act from this state of faith, you will be operating from a higher level of consciousness and any action or decision that comes from this will be more useful in the end.

Adaptability

> It is not the strongest of the species that survives, not the most intelligent that survives. It is the one that is the most adaptable to change.
>
> - Charles Darwin

It's vital that the leaders of today and the future have the ability to change their minds! I don't mean simply "I thought I was going to restructure one way, but I've decided to do it another way." I'm talking about the ability to have complete mindset shifts – i.e., the ability to suspend everything that you once thought was true about a topic and open your mind to a completely new way of viewing the topic.

This is a "light bulb moment" when your entire perspective changes. It's a clear requirement of a successful Leader because the world requires leaders who can do things radically differently for the future success of business as an institute as well as the continuation of the human race and the planet. No pressure!

In Jim Collins' book *Good to Great* he is trying to get the reader to shift their whole perspective on the topic of how companies change and grow effectively. He starts by saying:

> I want to give you a lobotomy about change. I want you to forget everything you've ever learned about what it takes to create great results. I want you to realize that nearly all operating prescriptions for creating large-scale corporate change are nothing but myths.

He needs the reader to have the ability to adapt their thinking – otherwise, what he goes on to say in his book will be read from the same level of thinking (the wrong level of thinking) that the reader had in the first place! He needs you to be able to literally open your mind to new concepts.

In this book, I am aiming to do the same for you as the reader. I am using a series of concepts to get you to open your mind: to become consciously aware of yourself as a human and how you work and to then be able to consciously decide what traits you want to draw on in any given Leadership situation. I am then asking you to run some new ways of thinking (which are the ways of thinking of people who are operating from a high level of consciousness) through your human system and to see if that helps you become a better leader. From all my research and field experience, it is my belief that these new ways of thinking and being, will lead you automatically to becoming a better Leader in ALL given circumstances – a bold statement and a big concept! So your ability to be adaptable is fundamental to getting the most out of this book.

A shift in a level of consciousness is an entire adaption, a mindset shift that affects everything in a leader's life, not just how you lead, but how you are in every context.

Excitement as well as the sudden realization of the new responsibility that a shift in consciousness brings is a common reaction for leaders who go through this transformation.

Leadership traits differ depending on your level of consciousness.

What you chose to do as a leader will depend on what you most value. If you value the people in your own tribe but not anyone else in the world, then you will be a Tribal Leader, still using the leadership traits discussed in this chapter. However, if you have reached a high level of consciousness, you will value all of humanity and therefore become a leader who may dedicate their life to world peace. Both leaders can be seen as using the same traits. So although personality traits are key differentiators between average and great leaders, we also need to recognize the different outcomes that leaders will use these traits to strive for, when they are coming from different levels of consciousness.

If we are at a survival level of consciousness that interprets the world to be a dangerous place and we are living in fear of not surviving, we will value leadership traits that are brutal in their approach to surviving. We will value a Leader who exterminates all other threats to the perceived limited resources that we need for ourselves (our tribe) to survive.

In this same vein, we have created heroes out of our leaders based on the level of consciousness that the majority of people in society are living from. We have championed leaders who beat down the competition at whatever cost, who gain the most money for their shareholders despite exploitation of others and global resources.

Jon Ronson is a British journalist who immersed himself in the world of mental health diagnosis and criminal profiling and wrote "The Psychopath Test: A Journey Through the Madness Industry" in 2011.

His book explores the traits of psychopathy, and although only 1% of the general population fit the criteria of a psychopath, Ronson found 4% of CEOs fit the criteria, making CEOs four times more likely to be psychopaths than people in other jobs!

When interviewed by Forbes Magazine, he states:

> Obviously there are items on the checklist you don't want to have if you're a boss. You don't want poor behavioral controls. It'd be better if you don't have promiscuous behavior. It'd be better if you don't have serious behavioral problems in childhood, because that will eventually come out. But you do want **lack of empathy, lack of remorse, glibness, superficial charm, manipulativeness.** I think the other positive trait for psychopaths in business is the need for stimulation and their proneness to boredom. You want somebody who can't sit still, who's constantly thinking about how to better things.

This belief that traits including a lack of empathy, lack of remorse, etc. are useful for business leaders, merely indicates the author's own level of consciousness and reflects the general beliefs of the business world today because the general population is operating from a certain level of consciousness that champions these behaviours in our leaders.

It is this mindset that I shift focus because I believe that leaders who do show empathy, remorse and do not demonstrate artificial charm or manipulative behaviours are more likely to build healthy, trusting relationships with their teams, their customers and investors. They will be "walking their talk" and unconsciously creating an organisational culture that displays the types of values that we come up with when brainstorming what we want our culture to be. They will also be creating an organisation that matches its brand proposition. The inside of the organisation will reflect the outside, so the world consumer base will also trust and believe in this organisation's products and services. What could be more powerful and financially successful than that?

Summary

I believe that the current mindset and therefore the "ways of doing business" bring money and power to a very small percentage of the human race and bring unpalatable results for much of the world's population. As the world's population has become more connected through the internet and more knowledgeable about what is going on, they will demand that you as as a leader operate from a higher level of consciousness.

I am suggesting that the return of these traits is drastically needed along with higher levels of consciousness. In the last few years we've seen the ramifications when leaders operate from other traits, when they have lied instead of having the courage to be honest, when they have only thought about what was best for themselves at the expense of many, when they have acted through greed and huge lapses of wisdom.

We've seen the results of world leaders acting from a base of fear, trying to control their own people or creating wars to protect their own country's economic position.

These people held leadership roles but were not demonstrating great leadership traits.

We are constantly disappointed in our leaders. Newspapers are quick to damn politicians (and recently bankers). However, we have all been part of the whole, so it's necessary to all take responsibility for raising our own game and connecting consciously to these traits, whilst still acknowledging our fears, frustrations and regrets.

Chapter Summary

In this chapter, I have covered the following topics:

- "What are the core Leadership traits that we admire and are likely to willingly follow?"
- How we all identify with certain core traits.
- The ability of great leaders to stay centered, clear thinking during challenging times or crisis.
- Ethical leadership is about being able to choose the right path for the greater good.
- The need for you as a leader to connect with your courage.
- The need for you as a leader to connect with your ability to have faith in yourselves, others and the path you are on.
- The requirement for leaders to be adaptable in their thinking and therefore in their actions.

In the next chapter, I will give a simple explanation of how we work as humans!

Once you are consciously aware of this as a leader, you will:

- Be able to use it to manage your own emotional reactions.
- Know how to affect the reactions of those around you.
- Have a most powerful advantage over leaders who are not consciously aware of this simple model.

CHAPTER 4

How We Basically Work

Introduction

This is a key chapter in the book, and if you could only read one chapter, then I would say this is the one to read! I demonstrate the following:

- How we basically work as human beings
- Why this is so useful to understand
- What you can use it for as a leader

How we basically work

Many people have written and talked about this concept. It is not a new phenomena to the human race. However, I wanted to try and explain it in simple terms to allow you, as leaders, to become consciously aware of it and therefore begin to chose to work with it, rather than be unconsciously ruled by it.

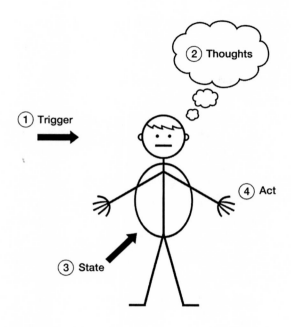

In the simple diagram above, there are four steps. In most cases, these steps run in chronological order from 1- 4. The process may run extremely fast, and we may not consciously be aware of most of it. So here, I'll slow down each step to explain how we work.

Step 1 – The event that kicks it all off – TRIGGER

We are designed like many other mammals to scan our environment for danger and react to keep ourselves alive. We have five senses – sight, sound, taste, smell and touch/feel – that all allow us to explore our physical environment.

If you watch a baby, they will pick up an object and try to use all five senses, including taste to understand what it is.

Because smell and taste are primarily connected to food, for our experience of the whole world around us we tend to use three main senses, sight, sound and touch/feel. The sense of touch/feel includes feedback from our whole body, not just our hands touching a new object.

Our bodies are designed to give us feedback about our external environment so that we can react and stay healthy and alive. We use our bodies to feel the physical environment such as temperature, changes in wind direction, humidity/dampness, etc.

We can also get feedback through our bodies about other people's energy. If we are centered enough in our own bodies, we can sense another person's sadness, anger or joy. We can also sense the presence of danger and probably the presence of compassion/love. Our gut reactions often tell us if someone or something is trustworthy, good or bad, right or wrong. We often speak of premonitions, and by that we mean that we have a feeling in our bodies that we're trying to interpret.

Our bodies have an internal feedback mechanism, too, through our nervous system. This is also designed to help us stay healthy and alive. Pain or discomfort brings our attention to that part of the body so that we can take action to heal ourselves.

If we ignore the feedback from our bodies, we do this at our own peril. Is there something that your body is trying to tell you through discomfort or pain that you are currently ignoring? If we do this for too long, the body will increase its level of discomfort or add other warning signs. Instead of ignoring our bodies or becoming annoyed with ourselves, I encourage my clients to welcome all feedback, to sit quietly with their eyes shut and ask, "What is my body trying to tell me here?"

Without pain, we have no true way of keeping ourselves safe. There are many stories of people with the rare congenital insensitivity to pain. Steven and Chris Pete, brothers born in 1983 and raised in Washington State, USA and both experienced lives without pain.

However, this condition often leads to many injuries and early death. Steven said in an interview:

> We grew up on a farm. My mum and dad tried to be protective without stifling my brother and me. But when you're out in the country, especially if you're a boy, you're going to go out and explore and get in a little mischief. So during my early childhood I was absent from school a lot due to injury and illness.
>
> Internal injuries are the ones I fear the most. Appendicitis is what really scares me. Usually whenever I have any type of stomach issues or a fever I go to the hospital just to get it checked out.
>
> *- BBC News Magazine*, July 2012

Constant feedback from the body is going on at an unconscious level, and we are only made aware of danger when we need to become conscious of it and therefore react to save ourselves. Our human design is still working for us in our modern environment. When we first meet people, we are unconsciously scanning to see if we can feel safe with them. We are asking "Are they from my tribe? Are they a threat or an ally? Are they a potential mate?"

Step 2 – The meaning we make in our minds – THOUGHTS

The next step is where the conscious mind (or the "executive mind" as some call it) makes meaning of the feedback from the five senses.

For example, if I am a hunter in the jungle and I see a movement out of the corner of my eye, I immediately stop to assess and see stripes move behind the jungle cover. My mind has a memory of these stripes from having seen a tiger. I can bring up the picture and compare it with what I see now. I can make a meaning of this change in my environment and if I make the meaning that the stripes are a tiger, then I will go through step 3 (STATE) and step 4 (ACTION) accordingly. If I think that it's a harmless animal, my STATE and ACTION will be remarkably different.

We have multiple pictures that we hold as memories based on our personal experiences. Often, something happens to illicit these old memory pictures and we make a meaning of what is currently happening based on these old pictures. In this way, we continue to interpret our life experiences from the original pictures that were laid down in our youth.

We are making meanings of our work environment (what we hear, how someone looks, what we feel in a meeting) all of the time. It is the meaning that we make of what is going on around us that leads us to experience a certain STATE, and based on that state, take a certain ACTION in the process.

Step 3 – How we feel in our bodies - STATE

The state we create for ourselves is determined by the meanings we make (the thoughts that run silently in our head). In my example above, if I think that the stripes are a tiger, then my brain will automatically give many signals to my body to mobilize it for survival. Adrenaline will be released, my muscles will tense, ready to spring into action, my heart rate will increase, etc. I may say I feel fear or excitement.

My body will move into a different state, depending on the meanings I make of what is happening around me.

If in a meeting, I see two of my colleagues exchange a look, I may interpret that to mean that they are not listening to what I'm saying and taking it seriously. Therefore, I may believe that I can't trust them to do what I think needs to be done to prevent something negative happening. With this interpretation, I may move to a state of anger.

Part of the success in the film *Crash* (2004), directed by Paul Haggis, is that each character behaves in a negative way in one set of circumstance, but a positive way in another. The characters are not just good or bad, but realistic. The film depicts a scene where a young boy hitches a lift. The driver and the boy start to make small talk, but the driver mistakenly believes the boy to be reaching for a gun, so he shoots him first! After killing the boy, he sees that what he was reaching for was a religious model of the Virgin Mary, not a gun at all.

Many classic dramas, including many of Shakespeare's tragedies and nearly all comedies, are based on incorrect thoughts that the players have about the meaning of something that happens. The final scene of *Romeo and Juliet* is littered with tragic misunderstandings. Greek and Roman mythology similarly use the misunderstandings of the players to create tragedy. Comedians lead us to think one thing, and when we realize that we have made an incorrect thought, we burst into laughter.

Often, incorrect meaning-making in the workplace leads to working relationships being strained, lack of trust and lack of open and honest dialogue. This is how mistakes are made, covered up or blamed on others and how organisations work in inefficient ways, still paying all their staff for a day's work, but only getting the equivalent of say 30% real productivity from them.

Step 4 – What we do/don't do - ACTION

This includes what I do, what I say, the tone of voice I use, my facial expressions and my body language.

Based on the THOUGHTS we are having and then the STATE we are in, we then take ACTION.

If, as you sit reading this book in a cafe, you suddenly think that the person next to you is about to steal your bag, you will act very differently than when sitting still and reading this book assuming your environment is perfectly safe!

Action is not just what you do, but it is also about your facial expression and the tone of your voice. It's what you say and even the emotion you are radiating into the world.

What can you use this model for?

It is only at the ACTION stag, that another person can observe what is going on for us. The TRIGGER, THOUGHTS and STATE are not observable to others. Nearly all traditional leadership training is focused on ACTION only – what leaders should do or say. However, what a leader does or says comes from the STATE that they are in, which in turn is generated by the THOUGHTS they are having about their environment/situation.

As a coach, people often tell me that they want to "do" x or stop "doing" y. I know that these actions or lack of actions are the result of my clients' internal processing of a TRIGGER, leading to certain THOUGHTS, leading to a certain STATE that then leads them to ACTION = do x or not do y. My role is to assist my clients to become consciously aware of what STATE they are in and what THOUGHTS they are having about the ACTION, so that they can then consciously decide to change what THOUGHTS they are running in their mind, which will then change their body's STATE (how they feel), and this will lead to a change of ACTION.

Our base operating thoughts

We all have general thoughts about life, people, the world, etc. Thoughts that sit as a base operating system in our minds. We run these basic thoughts and beliefs many times throughout our lives. These base-operating thoughts can be so ingrained that we are not consciously aware of them. If we shift some of these base-operating thoughts, then we fundamentally change our entire way of being. This is part of my work with leaders to enable you to first become consciously aware of your base operating thoughts and then shift them if they are no longer serving you.

How can we use this model to raise our consciousness?

We can raise our levels of consciousness as leaders by looking at these fundamental beliefs and consciously deciding if we want to keep running our entire lives from this base operating system or not.

Often, we only need to update our operating systems when we are faced with a problem that we can't seem to overcome. These problems have been created by the way we have been operating so far; simply doing more of what we've always done to overcome the problem only makes it worse.

For example, a client of mine recently stated that they were starting to make little mistakes but were worried that these would lead to bigger mistakes at work. They realized that they made mistakes because they were so tired. They were tired because they had spent the last 20 years driving themselves to work more intensely and for longer hours. Their immediate solution was to stay another hour at work to re-read all their documentation! This made sense to them because they have always overcome problems in the past by working harder and longer.

Case Study

I worked with a recruitment agency to help the leaders understand what their top sales person, Chris, was doing that enabled him to be so good. The leaders of the agency wanted to create a training course for the rest of the recruitment agents to enable them to become as good as Chris. I quickly discovered that the core difference between the other recruiters and Chris was his level of consciousness, or his mindset.

Chris came to work each day knowing that his purpose was to help people find jobs that they loved and help employers find the best people they could for their organizations.

He told me that he knew he was good at what he did. He loved it, and he felt that it was an important role to play in society because people spend so many hours at work. He wanted them to love what they did – just as he loved what he did. He understood that if people loved their work and worked in the right cultures, then they would be happy, successful and their organizations would be too. He often found jobs for his clients because he cared about them enjoying their jobs, too.

Chris' job satisfaction came from feeling that he had helped both the candidate and the employer, and he had several client relationships that lasted years because they just enjoyed working with him, and he always gave them the right types of candidates for their organization.

NOTE: Chris never focused on the commission he was earning. He viewed the money as an inevitable outcome from helping his clients. He held no fear around meeting his targets because his focus was on the day-to-day activities that would help his clients and candidates have more enjoyable working lives.

On the other hand, many of the lower performing recruitment consultants focused on billing their quarterly target amount. They spent far more time calculating how much they had billed and how much they still had to bill in order to achieve the targets that their managers had set them. They were more worried about not making target than being sacked. They were mainly operating from a state of fear, which was occasionally alleviated when they made a placement that contributed towards them reaching their target amount of money. They had not connected their daily work to a higher purpose; they just felt that they had to work to get money for their organization, and then they would similarly be rewarded.

Studies in the U.S. have proven that increasing the amount of money that an employee gets does not lead to higher performance. Often, it led to lower performance!

The difference between Chris and his colleagues was entirely based on mindset (THOUGHTS) that then affected the STATE that the recruitment agent was in most of the times. It was from this mindset (THOUGHTS) and STATE that they took ACTION each day.

For the other recruitment agents to shift their mindsets, they needed to stop focusing on their jobs as a way to earn money and commission for themselves, and start focusing on their job as a way to spend each day of the week, helping their clients and candidates become happier and more successful in their organisations and careers.

They needed to see a greater purpose and value for their role.

Chapter summary

This chapter is a key theoretical part of this book. Hopefully by now, you are more consciously aware of the following:

- How you basically work as a human being.
- By understanding how you basically work, you can decide to change the THOUGHTS you are running about a certain situation and therefore change your STATE and this will lead to you achieving a different ACTION and outcome.
- The practice of Conscious Leadership – all you need is a pen and paper to begin to write down the THOUGHTS you are running that are causing the STATE you find yourself in. From here, you can decide to run different THOUGHTS that will lead to a more desirable STATE and the ACTIONS you then decide to take as a leader will lead to a different outcome.

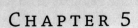

CHAPTER 5

How To Build Good Relationships

Introduction

In this chapter, I continue with the concept of how we work from Chapter 4 and explain the following:
- How we REALLY communicate through our STATES not our words
- That once we understand this, we can consciously decide to shift our STATE and begin to build better relationships
- An exercise to shift a relationship you currently have
- An exercise to build good relationships with your team

Highly conscious leaders not only take responsibility for their own reactions to their environment, they also know that they are responsible for how they relate to others.

We cannot be responsible for another person's thoughts, feelings or actions, only our own. However, when we are in a relationship – whether that be that a working relationship, a relationship with our customers, or our stakeholders – we are affecting the system.

As everything is connected in the universe, then we are constantly in relationship with everything. We are just not necessarily consciously aware of that. I discuss this concept later in the book.

For now, I want to explain the mechanics of how we connect to another person. Once leaders understand this, they have the power to decide to form much more productive relationships.

Is there someone you would like to have a better working relationship with? Someone who you just don't enjoy interacting with?

Most people leave their jobs, not for more pay, but because they don't have a satisfying relationship with their manager.

Each of us has the same basic way of working (TRIGGER – THOUGHTS – STATE – ACTION). Steps 1-4 were explained in Chapter 4. So if you put two people together you double the complexity. Both can trigger each other to have negative thoughts about the other person. This will cause both of them to create a negative state.

This phenomenon is how two people who have never met before can end up in a fight in a pub by the end of the night! John walks into the pub and looks at Mark standing at the bar. John may or may not be judging Mark, but Mark looks back and thinks he is being judged. Perhaps he starts to judge John, and now they are both creating a feeling of fear that may turn to anger. "What are you looking at?" asks Mark from a state of fear or anger because at some level he sees potential danger. This then escalates into a negative feedback loop of fear and aggression.

Exactly the same process occurs when two people fall in love. In this case, the meaning they make of each other is positive, they only see the positive (to begin with) and both feel states of trust, respect, calm and safety with each other. They both act from this state and begin to build a positive feedback loop.

In his book *Body Language: 7 Easy Lessons to Master the Silent Language*, James Borg stated that human communication consists of 93% body language and paralinguistic clues, while only 7% of communication consists of words themselves. If this is true, when I meet you, 93% of what I am communicating to you is based on the emotional state that I'm in. (I may not even be consciously aware that I am doing this, because I'm only consciously aware of what I'm saying). However, it is how I really feel about you/the situation that you will pick up, and not so much what I'm actually saying. In this way, we "read" people's truth about something, based on all the minute non-verbal signals that they are unconsciously giving us.

Have you ever experienced being with someone you know who is saying one thing but you are picking up the 93% of their communication and feeling a different thing? Their words don't match their perceived state? This leads us to confusion and lack of trust, because we know that their words don't match their state.

As a leader, whatever you do or say, others will pick up on your true state.

If you are totally adept at covering up your true state, people will pick up that you are hiding your true state even though they don't know what that is. This is incredibly unsettling for another human who is fundamentally designed to pick up the emotional state in others in order to make a judgment about how safe they are with that other person.

They will know that they can't 'read' you and feel anxious about this -- perhaps they'll keep asking you how you feel, or if you are happy/ok with x. They will not be able to fully trust you because you are blocking 93% of communication towards them.

It's not just the signs of non-verbal communication that we pick up, as we are hard-wired in our brains to attune to another person's physiology. In Daniel Goleman's book *Social Intelligence*, he describes an experiment between two psychiatrists and their patients. The first psychiatrist keeps interrupting the patient and doesn't seem to be listening to her. The second psychiatrist seems to be in tune with his patient who has just asked his girlfriend to marry him. They have been working for months on this patient's fears of commitment, so the fact that he has overcome them to propose is a triumph that both psychiatrist and patient share.

Both sets of psychiatrist and their patients wore a metal clip on their fingertip, which measures minute shifts in sweat responses. These wires were fed to a computer that produced a graph of lines showing the emotional shifts in all four players. The shifts between the first psychiatrist and his patient show a total disconnect. Their lines do not correspond, and they show high peaks and troughs. The emotional shifts between the second psychiatrist and patient, however, show a very similar path. The lines run up and down the emotional scale in harmony with each other.

"Until now neuroscience has studied just one brain at a time. But now two are being analyzed at once, unveiling a hitherto undreamed-of neural duet between brains as people interact," says Goleman.

How does this relate to leaders in business?

Goleman also cites a British study of health care workers who had two supervisors on alternate days. They dreaded interactions with one of the supervisors but enjoyed having the other supervisor work with them. On the days that the dreaded boss visited, the health care workers' average blood pressure jumped 13 points for the systolic and 6 for diastolic (from 113/75 to 126/81). While the readings were still in the healthy range, that much of an elevation, if maintained over time, could have a clinically significant impact. We are more likely to attune to the emotional state of our boss, or someone who holds power over us, because it is most important for our safety that this person is "happy" with us.

We are designed to adapt to our environment. Our environment includes the state (or energy) that those around us are emitting. That's because the emotional states we are in are unconsciously transmitted to those around us. If you are sensitive, you will intuitively know this and have been able to pick up other people's emotional states for years.

Honest verbal communication

This is where we need to understand that we have all been socialized differently. Even identical twins raised in the same family can have very different perceptions and reactionary thoughts to their external world.

So, once we are self-aware, we can use language to share with other people what we are thinking and feeling. This gives them a greater chance to react to our truth and therefore less chance of misunderstanding us.

In relationships that are not so good, we either hold negative beliefs about the other, and/or we think that they hold negative beliefs about us. We don't tend to verbalize our truth to the other person. We simply hold our judgment and look for more evidence to back that up!

In good relationships, we get to feel 'safe' with the other because they have told us what they are thinking and how they feel about external situations (including us). If we spend a long time with another person who is self aware and honest about what they think and feel and we do the same, we have the makings of a very good relationship (assuming that any negative judgments and misunderstandings have been resolved on both sides).

A Conscious Leader will understand that it's their state that will ultimately be communicated. They will consciously manage their state to genuinely be one of calm or excitement or whatever they truly want to communicate to the world. I have clients who will take a minute on their own to come back to calm before they act in any way. They may still be angry, but they can communicate this from a calm, centered place rather than acting out from an unconscious place. In this way, they engender trust and respect in those around them as well as create honest adult relationships.

Ultimately, it is your THOUGHTS at any one moment that will generate your STATE, and this is then communicated to the other. We tend to know when someone is thinking negative thoughts about us. We don't know exactly what they're thinking, but our bodies pick up on the level of mutual comfort or discord.

Non-judgmental listening

> Most of us rarely listen to what other people are saying. When we should be listening, we are responding to the impact of what we are hearing. In other words, we are listening to ourselves react.
> - Harville Hendrix, *Getting the Love You Want*

One of the first things that coaches learn is the art of being still in our own bodies and mind, and therefore being able to completely focus on what our client is saying. This act alone is hugely therapeutic for humans because simply being heard without being judged allows us to relax.

Once a leader has reached a level of consciousness that allows them to understand that fundamentally we are all connected (so I feel your pain and vice versa), then they are motivated to truly listen to their team, colleagues, stakeholders and customers because they know that this is the first step to good relationships.

Exercise for building good relationships with others

1) Think of someone with whom you would like to have a better working relationship, but for some reason you just don't like them, or just can't connect as well with them as you can with others.

2) Write down, off the top of your head, what you think about them. Be honest, as this is only for you to see. Make sure that you don't put their name at the top of the paper or make it obvious who it is in any way, in case you lose this information!

3) Next write down what you think they would say about you if a third party were interviewing them. Again, be honest. This is what they might say, even if you think they are incorrect.

4) Then mark at the side of each statement – from steps 2 and 3 – a negative sign if the thought is negative and a positive if the thought is positive.

5) Add up the number of negatives and the number of positives for each list. If you have more negatives than positives statements, this is what we need to change in order for the relationship to improve.

6) So letting go of your ego (to be right, to be better than this person), imagine you are them (sit in their shoes) and ask "What is my life like? How do I feel about myself? What am I fearful of? What do I love doing?"

7) Then, having a wider perspective on who they are and what is driving their behaviour, write some more positive statements about them – e.g.,, they are hard working, they are intelligent, they are just worried that they won't look good in the eyes of the boss etc.

8) How do you feel (in your body) towards this person now? Is there any shift? Write down how your state has now changed too.

9) Each time you interact with this person, ensure you have first read the list of positive statements and consciously shifted your state and/or read the list each day to re-set your state generally.

10) Do this exercise diligently for at least 5-10 interactions with this person, and see how they change towards you.

It only takes one person in a relationship to change their focus of thoughts towards the other to create a positive system, so if you really want to build a better relationship with someone, you need to focus on only the positives and build a conscious list of positive thoughts to start the ball rolling.

It helps if we realize that we might not know a person's personal history. We don't know why they behave and think as they do, but we do know it will be because of their socialization -- the lessons they learnt from their life so far. We are not all born into equal environments with equal chance to flourish in life.

Note: In the exercise above there is no need to say that any of the negative thoughts you initially had about them are untrue (because none of us are perfect). We have simply consciously refocused our THOUGHTS on the positive things. This then leads our STATE to become more positive too, and it is this STATE that the other person picks up unconsciously when they are with us, or interacting with us on the phone, or email, etc.

Exercise for building good relationships with your team:

Honestly answer the following questions and then have a look at the current THOUGHTS you are running about your team.

What are you grateful for in your team?

What do you most value about each member of your team?
(Do not get drawn into thinking about what you don't like about them!)

Is there anyone on your team that you feel will never make the grade?

Is it because of their level of consciousness? Is there anything you can do to help raise that? Do you have time as an organisation to do this?

Is it because you don't really connect with them? If so do the exercise above with them in mind.

Realize that you have the power (and responsibility) to create a high performing team. You can do this by consciously deciding to focus your THOUGHTS on positive things about your team members, your team's work, your team's contribution to the organisation and your team's potential to be really high performing.

Note: If you genuinely think that someone is really not performing because they just do not have the aptitude, then it is kinder to help them move onto a role where they will flourish. At the end of the day, most people want to feel that they are doing a good job. Is there an honest conversation you can have with this person? Have you avoided this conversation because you are afraid of their response?

Chapter Summary

By now, you will have had the chance to experience the shifts you can bring about in your relationships – not by trying to change the other person, or by telling them how they need to improve, but by simply changing your own THOUGHTS and therefore STATE that is then communicated to them.

This is a major practice of Conscious Leaders: deciding to take responsibility for their own THOUGHTS rather than staying stuck by blaming the other.

CHAPTER 6

How to Gain Control Over Your Emotional Responses

Introduction

In this chapter, I explain:
- Some of the common ways in which we stay disconnected from our difficult emotions – do you recognize any?
- What happens if we don't heed our body's warning signs!
- An exercise to connect to our bodies and emotions
- How our upbringing may lead us to judging ourselves for having certain emotions and try to deny or suppress them
- The ability to feel our emotions, not judge them, but take any useful information and move back to center – Ultimate Conscious Leadership

Have the courage to feel

First, we have to be prepared to really feel. If our thoughts lead to our emotional state then, when we feel an emotion, we need to be able to accept that emotion, and ask ourselves "What thoughts am I having right now that are leading me to feel like this?"

The path of the consciously-developed leader is ultimately one of courage because we tend to want to avoid any feelings of pain or suffering. If we are triggered to run thoughts that then lead us to feel something negative and to act from this place, then we will not get the results we really want in the world. To change this, we need to acknowledge the feelings that we have created.

Often, we are unconsciously triggered to run thoughts that we are not consciously aware of – which in turn will lead to a feeling in the body that we don't like! Instead of going through the process below, we try all sorts of activities to avoid having to feel the emotion.

Do you run these unconscious strategies – NOT to feel?

The behaviours we run so that we don't have to feel uncomfortable emotions are numerous. Some of the common ones include eating, drinking, shopping, working and cleaning. These behaviours are not a problem in themselves as they are often every day activities. However, if we find ourselves doing them compulsively or excessively, it is useful to stop and ask ourselves, "What is it I don't want to feel right now? Is it sadness, loneliness, despair, etc.? Will we survive if we just feel this for a few minutes and then say "Okay, now I know I can feel like this sometimes, and that's normal because everyone else feels like this sometimes, too."

We have many ways to distract our conscious minds from our feelings. On the Advanced Leadership Course I run, I ask participants to name all the ways we avoid keeping physically still and connected to our real feelings in the present moment. Here are some of the answers:

Drinking alcohol or taking drugs, socializing, watching TV, comfort eating, retail therapy, keeping busy, working, exercising to excess, having sex, internet surfing, Facebook, pornography, video game playing. This list is not definitive, but it gives us some of the methods we use for simply distracting ourselves from our emotions so that we either feel nothing, or temporarily feel something different.

So the first step is to have the courage to stop our particular distractions and be still, so that we can notice how we are feeling.

What happens if we don't heed the warning signs

Most of the time, our focus of attention is on the outside world, so we are less aware of what is going on inside our heads and our bodies. We may be so focused on the outside world and what we are doing, that we suddenly realize we are really hungry or that we needed to go to the bathroom some time ago and now our bodies are urgently giving us this message!

Often, we may have ignored signals from our bodies that we need to rest and reconnect to ourselves for so long, so our bodies decide to make us rest by causing some illness. We then have no choice, but to take time off from our "to do" list and lie still for a while.

As children, we were well-connected to our bodies, and we really felt things. But as we grew into adulthood and were forced to sit for long periods of time and simply use our minds, many of us became less connected to ourselves.

Bringing our focus of attention inside - Mindfulness

A huge shift for leaders wanting to raise their level of consciousness is to build in time during their day to bring their focus inwards. This allows them to use their mind to understand how their bodies feel; they consciously bring their bodies to a slower breathing pace, a more restful, still position (without falling asleep) and therefore begin to still the conscious mind too.

The process is almost the reverse of steps 1-4 in the diagram of How We Work. The exercise on mindfulness is set out below.

How to build the art of self-awareness

It is a real art to be able to be aware in the moment of your state and to be able to ask yourself, "What am I thinking in this situation that leads me to feel like this?" and "What happened to trigger these thoughts?"

To get to this level of sophistication takes practice. The practice commonly involves doing some form of meditation. There are many ways to practice being very self-aware in the present moment. The key component seems to be practicing being still and bringing your focus inside the body.

Taking the time (even two minutes a day) to do this should feel good because you are building a stronger relationship between your mind and your body. It is as if the body is an old, long-lost friend that we used to see and speak to every day but haven't really had the time for recently. We want to get back in contact and say "Hi, how are you?" and "What can I do to listen to you and respect you?"

As time goes by, Conscious Leaders develop the ability to spend most of their waking hours with part of their conscious awareness focused internally on their bodies. Some of the things you can do that will help develop this relationship between your mind and your body are the following: yoga, martial arts, dance, meditation, being still and silent in nature and mind/body therapies.

Some of my clients set conscious reminders to check in with their bodies – e.g., each time they stop to have a drink, they will stop and ask themselves "How do I feel in my body right now? What state am I in?" Others set an alarm on their phone to remind them 5-10 times a day to re-connect. It only takes a second to decide to take your focus from everything outside of you to everything inside of you.

If we do something new in life enough times over, our brains develop new neurological pathways, and we eventually become totally competent in the new activity. A great example of this is learning to drive. Initially, we drive very consciously, thinking about each step we need to take to drive effectively. However, once we've driven consciously enough times, our brains just develop a "knowing" of how to drive, and we continue to drive without having to think about it. We have built new neurological pathways in our brains and become unconsciously competent. This is obviously different from being completely unconscious!

Learning self-awareness follows the same pattern. So although it may take a couple of weeks of consciously bringing your focus inside to how your body feels, after a short while, you will just be self-aware without needing consciously to do this exercise.

Exercise – To Bring Our Focus Inside - Mindfulness

1) Ideally, give yourself plenty of time – at least 1 hour.
2) Find a place that is peaceful and where you won't be interrupted.
3) Turn off your phone and all other gadgets that could interrupt this exercise.
4) Close your eyes and bring your focus to your own breathing, then to all areas of your body starting with toes and going upwards to the top of your head.
5) Notice how your breathing has slowed down. Notice any resistance to the exercise (the conscious mind trying to stay in control by interrupting this process telling you it's a waste of time and so forth.)
6) In your mind's eye, imagine that you are moving gently inward down into your body and find yourself in a beautiful place where you are just resting. In this place, notice your deep slow breathing. Decide what you want to draw into your body with each inhale (e.g., energy, compassion, peacefulness). Decide also what you'd like to breathe out of your body on each exhale, what do you want to let go of? (e.g., anger, jealousy, fear). Just stay here breathing for as long as you wish.

7) Whenever you want, you can return in your mind's eye to the surface and open your eyes and come back to focusing on the outer world.

Remember you can bring your focus back inside of yourself to this beautiful place of rest and rejuvenation whenever you want to. Know that if you practice this at least once a day, you will be able to go there within seconds at any time you choose.

Getting the message from our feelings

Because our nervous system gives us feedback about possible physical harm through feeling pain so that we can keep our physical bodies healthy and alive, then perhaps our feelings give us feedback so that we can keep ourselves healthy and alive from a psychological perspective.

Anger

If something causes me to be angry, then often the thoughts t running through my mind are telling me something that is wrong with this situation for me. My anger may be the first thing that I'm consciously aware of. I may then have to stop and ask myself, "Wow, what am I thinking that is making me angry in this situation?"

There will be a huge amount of information in the answer that is valuable to understand. Once I understand why a situation has caused me to be angry, I may be grateful for having this angry feeling as it was giving me a valuable warning sign. I may also decide to do something different in the world or try and make the world a better place because of my anger.

I may realize that my anger is really based on my own beliefs and insecurities that I can address in my own thought system – e.g., "Do I really need to be angry that this person cut in front of me in their car? Do I really care? They obviously feel the need to push in front of me in this moment but I don't need to compete with them. I don't need to rush and feel stressed, etc."

By simply being aware of the thoughts running through my head, I may become aware of a deeper base thought – e.g., "I am angry that this person has cut in front of me in their car because I feel that I'm always pushed out of the way. I feel like this at home and at work. I can see different triggers, all triggering the same feeling because they are reinforcing a core belief that I've been holding for nearly all my life."

> Anybody can become angry - that is easy, but to be angry with the right person and to the right degree and at the right time and for the right purpose, and in the right way - that is not within everybody's power and is not easy.
>
> -Aristotle

Fear

Often behind our anger is a feeling of fear. It's useful to ask, "What is it I'm really afraid of here?"

Our fear is a warning sign from the body to tell us that we've run thoughts or pictures of something that may happen in the future that could cause us harm. Fear is always about the future, even if it is a thought about what might happen in the next minute. We cannot be afraid of what has already happened in the past. We can keep running a trauma in our mind and getting the feelings we had at that time again and again (in fact that is often how we process something frightening that has happened to us). However, unless we imagine that it could happen again in the future, we can't be fearful of it.

Once we understand what thoughts or pictures we've been triggered to run, we can use this information wisely to do something to help mitigate the perceived risks. Or we may again realize that our fear is generated by thoughts about our own insecurities and decide to consciously change those thoughts – e.g., "I'm afraid that if I lose my job, I won't get another one, I'll become poor and my loved ones will leave me." Is this realistic? Another thought could be "If I lose my job, I will have my savings to live on and I'll get another job within 3/6 months which I might like more than this one anyway."

We fear violence less than our own feelings. Personal, private, solitary pain is more terrifying than what anyone else can inflict.

-Jim Morrison

Sadness

We are currently living in a time when to be sad or to admit to being sad is not really that socially acceptable. We are often given the message that we should always be happy and if we are not happy then that is our own fault, and we need to search for what will make us happy and get rid of the things that are making us sad. This in itself contributes to a lot of unnecessary suffering. If we could just accept that sadness is one of the emotions of life – that we are going to feel from time to time – we would probably be better off as a society.

You cannot protect yourself from sadness without protecting yourself from happiness.

-Jonathan Safran Foer

Sadness is a necessary emotion for us to process change and move on to new things. We need to acknowledge what we've lost in order to grow and develop. To develop through dealing with the loss of those we love is part of the cycle of life. If everything stayed the same and we never felt the loss of something, we'd never grow.

It is important to accept and appreciate our ability to be sad. It is also an emotion that takes a physical toll on the body, so if we don't acknowledge our sadness (and are trying to suppress this uncomfortable feeling by keeping busy, or medicating ourselves with alcohol, etc.), then we can cause our bodies to break down in some way.

Often when we are sad in life, we need to take time out to rest, stay quiet, allow ourselves the privacy to cry, and be held by a close loved one. If we stay connected to our body and understand what we need in any given moment, the wisdom in the body will help us move through this period of sadness (be it a moment, a day or a few years of grieving for a loved one). We will allow the energy to flow through us, and at some point, we will have processed our loss and have the ability to adapt to a new life.

When we become aware of the constant negative thoughts we have been running about ourselves, we may become sad for the pain we have caused ourselves all these years. It may be important to grieve for the person you were, so that you can transform to a new level of consciousness.

People in organisations go through these emotions during an unwanted loss (especially if they feel that it was out of their control) such as a round of redundancies. It is important to understand their need to discuss how they feel, reminisce about the 'good old days' and miss those colleagues that have gone. This is all part of their way of processing the change. Its also important for leaders to understand that during this process, productivity will probably dip because energy is being used to process loss, rather than being externally focused on the day-to-day business.

When organisations constantly change their structures and processes without entire buy-in from staff, they are actively lowering the productivity of their staff because they are sending them again and again through an emotional journey of grieving for loss as well as having the learn the "new way."

Experiencing our emotional responses and coming back to calm

We are designed to feel the full range of possible emotions (based on what we choose to think about any given situation). We are also designed to experience an emotion and then come back to a place of calm.

The flexibility to feel an emotion, acknowledge it and then bring ourselves back to a calm, centered state is one of the art-forms of the consciously developed leader.

They take total responsibility for their own emotions (rather than blame others and/or external factors for them). They understand the value of their body's feedback, so honour all their emotions. They can then move consciously to a more centered/grounded place. This doesn't mean that they no longer feel the initial emotion but it means that the emotion has not consumed them, they are able to think clearly and act in the world from this base (not acting out, such as uncontrolled shouting).

The Dalai Lama states in his book *The Art of Happiness*, that finding meaning for our suffering is a powerful way to cope with the ordeals that life throws at us. However, he warns that we must cultivate a meaning for suffering when we are in relatively good times because "a tree with strong roots can withstand the most violent storm, but the tree can't grow roots just as the storm appears on the horizon."

He also says that while at times suffering can serve to toughen us (what doesn't kill me, makes me stronger), it can also serve to soften us, to make us more sensitive and gentle. "The vulnerability we experience in the midst of our suffering can open us and deepen our connection with others."

Emotional resilience and self-management are vital to good Leadership.

Basic Emotions

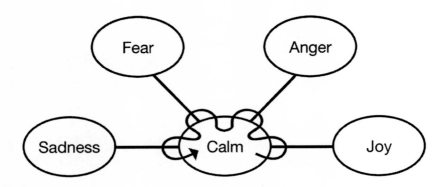

The emotional groups illustration depicts the basic emotions we experience as animals in order to help us stay alive and fully experience life. This diagram, therefore, doesn't include emotions that are based on self-judgment like, guilt, shame or inadequacy. These emotions are secondary responses to feeling one of the four groups of emotions above – e.g., if I feel angry, I may then judge myself for feeling anger as I have been taught that I should never feel anger, so I then feel shame. The trouble with this secondary judgment is that we often just feel the secondary judgment and cannot get to the first feeling, in order to process it properly. This way our basic animalistic emotional responses get repressed again and again.

The words sadness, fear, anger and joy are the generic terms in the model to represent all the other terms we use.

Fear may be expressed at work by people saying, "I'm anxious or concerned about this project," or "This doesn't sit right with me for some reason," or "I'm just not sure I trust this person."

Anger may be expressed at work by people saying: "I'm just really frustrated with x," or "I can't believe this project is so awful," or "It's just typical of management to do/say y."

Sadness may be expressed at work by people reminiscing about how good the "old days" were, or wishing that someone was still here, or something was still how it used to be. They may say, "I'm just over it," "I'm tired with it all," or 'I'm disappointed'.

I use this model for coaching leaders to show how the human body is designed to feel any one of these emotions but to then extract any useful information that the body is bringing them and consciously come back to a calm center. One of the easiest ways to come back to a calm center is to take a deep breath and to think, "This will pass, it's just a strong emotion."

What happens if we get stuck?

Other animals seem to feel the basic survival emotions and naturally come back to calm. They may be in fear one moment but as soon as the trigger is removed, they go back to calm – like a wild rabbit that stops and freezes when we walk too close to it. But as soon as the potential danger has moved further away, the rabbit resumes eating the grass in apparent calm.

Humans, however, can get in the way of this natural process by denying or judging our own emotions. We can feel fear and yet be so unaware of it that we stay stuck in a state of perpetual anxiety. At an unconscious level, we are trying to avoid dealing with our anxiety, so we just stay busy or distract ourselves in other ways so that we can deny our true feeling.

We can become stressed about something that is not within our control. This means that there is nothing we can do in the external world to create a place of calm for ourselves. The only thing we can do is become self-aware of the fact that we feel stressed, understand the trigger, realize that we have no control over this and decide to consciously stop running the thoughts that created our stress in the first place. We may instead run thoughts like "This is out of my control, so there is no point in worrying about it" or "I will deal with this if it happens, but for now, I choose not to think about it."

We may feel anger and then add even more anger to our system by feeling angry with ourselves for getting angry! We can use our powerful thoughts to generate a secondary emotional reaction to our initial emotion. So it's also important to ask, "I know that I feel really anxious about that but how do I feel about being really anxious?" Often we judge our own emotions.

This adds a level of complexity to our system and means that the consciously developed leader must cultivate absolute self-honesty. What I mean by this is truly aiming to be honest about what you think and how you feel, even if that is simply being honest with yourself. This allows you to start questioning your own beliefs and slowly change the way you see yourself, others and the world. This shift in beliefs ultimately leads you to raise your level of consciousness.

"Everything's always great" syndrome

Often, we are raised with the unrealistic expectation of ourselves that we can always be happy. When we are not feeling happy, we can think that there must be something "wrong" with us! This is exhausting as we have to hide all our feelings apart from joy and keep up the show of joy. Being a good leader doesn't mean always being up beat, it means being real and allowing your people to connect to you and trust you because they know you are going through the same emotional challenges as they are. As a group, you know you can stay centered and still move towards your goals. All emotions pass – they are transitory – but we can learn from them and understand their message/value with gratitude.

Chapter Summary

When a leader simply acts out from anger, shouts and stamps their feet, they lose credibility. To understand and accept your fear, then move to a centered state and still go forward, is an act of courage, and this way of being as a leader will be admired and respected.

> "We first have to learn how negative emotions and behaviours are harmful to us, and how positive emotions are helpful. And we must realize how these negative emotions are not only very bad and harmful to one personally but harmful to society and the future of the whole world as well."
> -Dalai Lama and Howard Cutler, *The Art of Happiness.*

So by now, you have:

- Realized some of the unconscious ways in which you were avoiding your emotions.
- Become aware of the emotions that you may be unconsciously judging and any secondary emotional responses you have.
- Learned a simple exercise you can do to connect to your emotions and stay with yourself through challenging emotions like loneliness, panic or despair.
- Gained an understanding that the Conscious Leader feels all these emotions, but is ok with them, can accept them and then come back to center before acting.

In the next chapter, I give you some ways of thinking that may rapidly shift your level of consciousness.

CHAPTER 7

How To Reprogram Your Operating Systems

Introduction

In this chapter, I share:

- How we came to have our unconscious beliefs
- An exercise on how to shift your mindset around who you are
- How to develop through others – whole of life is a training program if you want to keep learning about yourself!

Once we are connected enough to our bodies we can know at any moment how we are feeling. Then, we can track that feeling back and ask, "What thoughts am I running that are generating this feeling?"

In NLP (Neuro-Linguistic Programming, an epistemology developed by John Grinder and Richard Bandler), there is a concept that we have universal beliefs. These are beliefs that are so regularly applied and fundamental for us that they sit like a base operating system in our thinking mind.

In order to develop my own practice as a Leadership Coach, it has been necessary for me to understand the core universal beliefs and practices of some of the most highly developed people that have written about how they see the world and what they think about the universe, the human race, the meaning of life, etc.

These may be heavy subjects that we don't want to be bothered thinking about. However, in Chapter 8, I wanted to share a few of the mindsets that seem to help people raise their levels of consciousness and therefore become entirely transformed leaders. Firstly, I want to explain how we can consciously decide to change the thoughts that we habitually have.

Shifting our own insecurities

> The mind holds on through beliefs, expectations, and interpretations. It takes a lifetime to build up these conditioned responses, but dismantling them occurs moment by moment. When you find yourself in a situation in which you are certain of disaster, loss, hurt, or any other negative outcome, use [the following formulas] as appropriate:
>
> My fears may come true, but the outcome will not destroy me. It may even be good. I'll wait and see.
> -Deepak Chopra, *The Path To Love*

Those that are highly consciously developed do understand the human condition. They have often gone through the classic psychological development steps and moved towards levels 5 - 7 in Richard Barrett's model of consciousness. (Chapter 16).

At a basic level, we all just want to survive and be happy but we also want to grow and develop ourselves in the world and feel fulfilled with how we are using this experience on earth. In order to move from the "survive and be happy" mode of operating, we will need to take risks and the very act of growing and developing in the world may threaten what we initially thought was a way to stay safe (have the physical body survive) and be happy (get our physical and emotional needs met).

It is at this juncture in our lives, when the body wants one thing and the soul wants another, that we can feel pulled in two different directions. Two different voices say, "Stay safe/your responsibilities mean you can't change," but also "Take a risk, life isn't about being safe!". This can result in what is commonly known as a "mid-life crisis."

Highly consciously developed leaders have gone through this dilemma, faced up to it and taken the risks. They have moved beyond the need to have the bulk of their attention focused on their own survival and their own emotional needs. Instead, their attention is mostly focused on their purpose in the world and living each day in service to others. This sense of service is very different from the service we may give to those around us through a sense of duty and guilt because of our socialization. As in the example of the recruiter, James, who served his clients and candidates in the recruitment agency from a sense of pure joy because his purpose was connected to it, rather than serving through a sense of duty or merely being paid to do it and feeling he "should" do it, or he would lose his job.

Those at higher levels of consciousness believe that we are all the same at this basic level and that our actions are just the product of us doing what we think is best for ourselves in that particular moment. They hold base-operating beliefs about people such as "we are all just doing our best on our own personal development journeys with the tools that we have."

The effects of our socialization

The general theory is that when we were born we were like a clean slate and had no beliefs. As we start to socialize, we picked up many different messages about ourselves, others and the world which become engrained in our belief systems like core operating beliefs.

Many of the beliefs we hold about ourselves are due to the reaction or words of the adults that raised us. This includes our main caregivers, teachers, close friends or family members, etc.

We seem to grow up with insecurities about ourselves, our personalities and/or our potential to do well in the world.

Perhaps this is partly due to the fact that we are socialized above all to fit in. Because humans are social animals, we need to fit into our tribe in order to survive. Any perceived threat to us not fitting in, or being unloved, will trigger fear in us as children, so we hide anything about ourselves that we believe won't be accepted and we begin to unconsciously mold ourselves to become what we think we should be and comply with what we think we should do.

This phase of socialization is essential. Without it, we would not be able to identify with our group and may be totally ostracized from society. However, this socialization can come at a cost.

Many of us grow into adults with what the coaching industry has termed "limiting beliefs." A limiting belief is a negative belief about who we are and what it's possible for us to do – e.g., "I'm not very clever" or "I'm lazy" or "There's something wrong with me" or "I'm not good enough." There are many different forms of these negative beliefs, but in Ben Renshaw's book *Successful but Something Missing,* he sets out some of the common negative core beliefs that people have incorporated in their childhood.

Often, when we start to practice greater self-awareness by focusing on how we feel, what thoughts generated that feeling and what the trigger was, we start to uncover these negative and therefore limiting beliefs about ourselves.

Consciously developed Leaders will have uncovered a lot of their own negative beliefs and accepted that these beliefs were simply a product of their misunderstanding about themselves that they picked up unwittingly in their earlier years. They believe that these thoughts are just the product of their socialization. Therefore, they take full responsibility for themselves and know that ultimately they can choose not to have these thoughts and to vigilantly "weed them out" when they catch themselves thinking them again.

By beginning to shift our mindset from one of self-criticism, self-judgment and self-hatred to a mindset of self-acceptance, self-compassion and self-love, we are raising our level of consciousness.

Leaders operating from a high level of consciousness have personally developed to be more accepting of their own ability to become anxious or angry and act from that base. In accepting their own frailty simply as a human experience, they will automatically have acceptance and compassion for others.

How does this help the leader lead their people in times of change or crisis?

The leader is called upon to (a) be consciously aware of other people's states, (b) to consciously manage their own state, so that they are regularly coming back to a calm centered state, and (c) to have compassion for those around them who are acting from states of fear and anger rather than judging them or looking down on them.

The awareness that they themselves could easily be acting in the same way is the humility that helps leaders stay grounded and respectful to those they lead.

Exercise for shifting mindset on who you are

Nothing is perfect, so could you accept some things that you cannot change and focus on what is really good about you as a leader?

What are your top 5 personality traits that make you a good Leader?

(Note: We are all human and although we tend to groups of personality traits. We have the potential to have ALL personality traits. So even the greatest leaders knew that they had things about them that were not ideal. They were okay with that. What could you accept about yourself and be okay with?)

What can you do about developing yourself as a leader?

Close your eyes and notice your breathing, ask your body gently, "What do I need right now?"
Let whatever the first answer or images that come to mind be the correct answer.

(Note: Often, the message is "rest" or a picture of a beach because high achievers are those people who push themselves and are most likely to become leaders in hierarchical organisations. They are likely to ignore their body's feedback signals of exhaustion.)

Close your eyes and breathe deeply. Know that you can ask your "higher self" or "wise self" any question. An answer will come to you either by thought, picture, or realization of another sort. If an answer doesn't come straight away, have faith that sooner or later something will happen, someone will say something, you will see, or think, something and know that that is your answer.

Learning to develop through others

Often, what we judge and dislike in another is the very trait that we could also have, but totally deny. We all have the capacity to display every trait and experience every state, but we are trying to hide or simply not experience the traits that we think are unacceptable.

When we see this trait displayed by others, we judge them as unacceptable (as we have unconsciously judged ourselves at some point in our lives). The diagram below shows an illustration of the types of personality traits that may fall into each group.

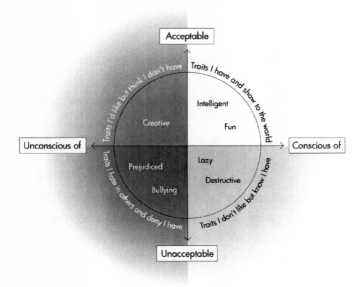

Highly conscious Leaders understand this and so take responsibility for their own negative judgments of others. They realize that it's only something in themselves that they have not come to terms with that is creating their dislike of the other person.

They realize that the challenge of having a good working relationship with this person that they struggle to appreciate is a perfect opportunity for them to develop a part of themselves!

Personal development is a continuous way to shift towards self-acceptance and self-appreciation. Once we have built a good relationship with all of our own personality traits and ways of being, then we automatically have compassion for others.

The more your judgments of yourself softens and you begin to be okay with who you are, the more you will begin to accept others. Your first relationship is with yourself; if this is good, then you can relate well to others and to the outer world. If your relationship with yourself is not so good (e.g., if you're beating yourself up for not being good enough, clever enough, working hard enough, etc.), then you will struggle to be a good leader.

This is not to say that as a leader you just go around with rose tinted glasses thinking everyone is being honest with you. A wise leader will have compassion and understanding towards those who lie, cheat, steal, etc. They may decide calmly not to tolerate it and take action, but they will not react emotionally because they hold a broader view of people's capability. They may think, "I know this person has lied to me but it's not personal. They just think that lying to me is their best option." They haven't yet developed to a higher level of consciousness and emotional maturity. When we truly accept that we (and all people) can also be dishonest, lazy, greedy, bullying etc at times, then we see the world more clearly, without taking other people's ways so personally.

We know that all people (including ourselves) have the potential to display all traits. We forgive ourselves (and everyone else) for this human predicament. We raise our consciousness to a different level, one of greater wisdom and compassion.

When we can consciously choose how we want to be in each moment, then we are reaching self-mastery and will be seen by the outer world as being centered, calm, compassionate, wise, etc. If you lead from this position, people will want to work with you because it will feel good for them to be in your company.

Chapter Summary

At the end of this chapter, you should have a better understanding of how you have gained some of the core beliefs that you run about yourself, other people, work, the way the world works, etc.

You will understand that we all have some form of negative belief but you can CONSCIOUSLY shift yours bit by bit by staying self-aware and running these mindset-shift exercises.

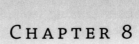

CHAPTER 8

Experience Higher Levels of Consciousness

Introduction

In this chapter, I set out:

- Some of the core operating beliefs of leaders who are operating from high levels of consciousness. If you are not already viewing the world through this lens, then I invite you to "try on" these beliefs and see what difference that could make to you as a Leader.
- Core operating beliefs of leaders at lower levels of consciousness and the impact that this has.

We intuitively look to people who we feel are operating from a higher level of consciousness from us and want to spend time in their company. It is as if we are trying to catch their way of thinking and being, and actually, this is a very good way to raise our own levels of consciousness and develop as leaders.

I have set out below some of the core operating beliefs that leaders have who are operating from a high level of consciousness. I also compared the beliefs of those leaders operating at a lower level of consciousness to help you see the difference. You may already recognize that you are operating with these core beliefs, but if not, it might be helpful to just "try on" the new belief, or way of seeing the world, and notice if this makes a difference to your emotional state and therefore your actions as a leader.

This is the quickest way I know to help leaders first experience what it is like to operate from a higher level of consciousness. Somehow, because it feels so much better and allows for such greater results, my clients seem to keep practicing this way of seeing the world, until it becomes their automatic mindset.

Note for Coaches: When I am working at the group level, running a Leadership or Coaching Training course, I am consciously holding these Core Beliefs to ensure that my state is relaxed, calm, compassionate, etc., which is the energy field that I want to consciously create for those in my courses. It is because I also believe that we learn best and can get breakthroughs into the next levels of consciousness when we are sitting in this type of energy field.

Scarcity v. abundance mindset

Someone operating from a scarcity consciousness has probably unconsciously learnt that "there isn't enough for me." Leaders from this mindset will never have enough. They will feel anxious to be earning more and more money and drive their organisations to produce more and more profit. They will often be emotionally demanding, expecting staff to stay late and be as committed as they are, yet will be angry if other people don't share their view of what's important in the world.

On the other hand, often those who reach the highest levels of consciousness think that they only really need the very basics to sustain their human body and emotional connections. They no longer crave more and more material possessions, and they will often choose what they consume based on what is best for the resources of the planet.

Those leaders who are operating from the fear that they won't get their own needs met often feel that they need to fight to get their share. This is a mentality of scarcity. A leader with this level of consciousness will have many things in their environment that trigger them to make meaning (THOUGHTS) that "there's not enough" or "I won't get enough." This then creates a STATE of anxiety and possibly anger in order to fight to get their share. We can all regress to this level of consciousness if we perceive our environment to be one of survival (an environment in which we have to fight to survive is one that if we don't fight, we may die).

Some organisations foster a culture of survival level of consciousness by suddenly firing their staff for perceived failures. A round of restructuring and redundancies will also trigger many people to feel that they are working in an environment where they may not survive.

Many staff (including some of the leaders) may be spending much of their time at work in a state of anger or fear (fight or flight mode).

It is at this point that a Conscious Leader is most required.

Those acting from a scarcity mentality will automatically be competitive because in their world there is a limited amount of everything, and they need to compete and beat others to get their share and survive. Their world is a "dog eat dog" world of fear and survival. Their energy and focus will be on beating the competition rather than simply doing their best. Their motivation for work will be fear (fear of failure, not getting what they need), rather than being motivated by a genuine desire to help improve the lives of their customers (be that internal or external).

Leaders operating from a scarcity mentality will feel better (a moment of relaxation from fear) when others fail. They are likely to create silos within their organisations because their competitiveness extends not just to other organisations but towards their own peers to race for the top job.

If people acting from this level of consciousness feel that they are not "winning" and therefore not getting their share, they will become aggressive – either against themselves (beating themselves up to try harder, do more hours, more work, beat more people) or they will become aggressive towards others because they will blame others for taking their share.

This mindset is hugely disempowering. It's a belief that "I've tried my best to get my share and I've failed. That means not only am I a failure, but others have beaten me and taken my share. This then means that they had the power to choose to voluntarily give me my share, but as I assume they have the same mindset as me, they have kept everything for themselves."

A lot of energy in business is wasted by leaders and employees looking at what the competition is doing and fearing that they will "get ahead." Energy is wasted beating themselves up through fear that "we've got to work harder than the competition to survive." This type of leadership thinking leads to fear/anger and a blame-based culture. These organisations are hugely inefficient because their key resource, the energy focus and creativity of their staff, is hindered when people are in a state of fear/anger and therefore taking actions to blame others or cover their backs.

The opposite of a scarcity mentality is an abundance mentality. This is the base belief that there is an abundance of whatever you need (money, love etc.).

Those that live from this mindset act very differently. They are less often triggered to fear and so do not act from fear. They tend to be generous and attract generosity in return. They tend to trust that there will be enough for them because they believe that there is enough for everyone. Their THOUGHTS run something like this: "There is an abundance of clients, customers and business opportunities, I just need to connect with them."

They don't need to focus so much of their energy on what others around them have got, because to them, it's irrelevant. There is enough for everyone.

A leader who has an abundance mentality will not bother to try and beat the competition because there is enough for everyone. They won't be ignorant of their competition because they can learn from their competitors' mistakes but they will put more of their focus on what they can do for their own customers (because they believe that "what goes around, comes around"). They will focus on how they can best serve their customers and contribute in the world.

There is no fear in giving because there is an abundance of energy, money, clients, etc. – "I can give and give and I'll just get more and more back." This leader will be in a state of calm, centered excitement about what they can do for their customers. They will encourage their staff to think creatively and come up with new ways to serve their customers (as opposed to encouraging their staff to think of new ways to take money from their customers).

The state that they and their staff work in is one of calm, centered, and of creativity. This is the ideal state for innovation, collaborative teamwork and a genuine, customer-centered approach to business.

Customers will sense this too and ironically may transfer from an organisation that is operating from a scarcity mentality to one operating from an abundance mentality. Thus, the outer world again reflects the reality of the thoughts that each leader holds. The leader with a scarcity mentality can turn around and say "You see, there are only so many customers in this market and they are going to the competition. We have to do what we've been doing, but even more of it, to win them back!"

The organisation led by a consciously developed leader with the abundance mindset will not only be much more enjoyable to work in (so will attract top talent), but it will also be an organisation that is pleasurable to interact with (so attracting customers, investors and business opportunities). It will also be an innovator in the market place and will therefore unconsciously be always beating the competition (even though the people of this organisation didn't invest much of their time focusing on doing so!). How frustrating for the leader with the scarcity mindset!

Just by shifting your mindset as a Leader, you will completely turn your organisation around.

Read the statement below a couple of times:

> It feels energizing to work in this organisation, we have great leaders and staff. There is an abundance of opportunity for us right now and we are positioned to provide great value to the market place with our innovative products and services so we can't fail to grow revenue in return.

What would it be like to think this every day even as you handle challenges along the way?

How would this change your team and organisation?

Business exists to serve society not the other way round

When I start to work with the Leadership Team of any organisation I ask, "What is your vision?" or "What are your current organisational goals?" Often the answer is something like "to double our profit in 2 years" or "to increase revenue by 10%."

These aren't visions or even SMART goals. I think to myself, "no wonder the people who work in this company don't feel as if they are making a difference in the world."

Goals or visions that simply focus on how much money an organisation can make have missed the point. A vision by definition is visual. You need people (staff, investors, etc.) to be able to picture something that feels worthwhile and achievable, when you tell them about the vision for your organisation.

If leaders make money their goal, and simply focus on profit, then their customers and staff will pick up on this. They will know that the leaders are simply out to make money and not in business to help their customers. Unfortunately, it feels as if this is now the general state of affairs in the Western business world. Customers, employees and other stakeholders do not trust business leaders to have their best interests at heart. Employees are quick (and rightly so in many cases) to believe that the leaders are only in it for themselves and what they can get out of the company. Customers are quick to believe that corporations are only in it for themselves and what they can get out of the customer.

A statement around doubling profit is really just the measurement of another vision or goal, which should be about giving value to the customer or the world in some way.

In capitalism, if you provide value to society in some way, then society shows their appreciation of this value through the use of money. So if your organisation is providing value to the world in some way, you can rest assured that the money will flow into your organisation as a result of this.

Therefore, as leaders, there is a need to shift your mindset from focusing on the money you have made in the last quarter and the money you think you will make in the next quarter, and simply focus on what you can do to improve the world (either improve your customers' lives or actually improve the state of the world). To genuinely do this takes courage because we have been engrained in a culture where to NOT focus on the money would seem outrageous. Whenever I speak to leaders about this particular mindset shift, I receive the largest amount of skepticism and fear.

Successful leaders in today's society get this, though. Richard Branson said recently in an interview:

> To get a sense of where you could improve and innovate in your own company, try buying your company's products or services incognito, then try using them. If you run into a problem, get in touch with customer relations – assuming, of course, that you can track down the contact information, a page that is usually hard to find on most websites. Throughout this process, take notes and take names. When you're done, follow up and review with your team: What changes or innovations would make your product or service not only more useful to your customers, but more memorable and enjoyable? Were the interactions with customer service representatives of the sort that you would like your customers to have? How could they be more helpful?

"Leaders exist to serve the greater good, not themselves," Jim Collins states in an interview about his book *Good to Great*. In his words:

> At a deeper level, we found that for Leaders to make something great, their ambition has to be for the greatness of the work and the company, rather than for themselves. That doesn't mean that they don't have an ego. It means that at each decision point—at each of the critical junctures when Choice A would favor their ego and Choice B would favor the company and the work—time and again the good-to-great Leaders pick Choice B.

Today's world uses the terms "ethical leadership" and "integrity" to describe leadership from this mindset. What we are really talking about are leaders who are secure enough in themselves to take a risk and do the right thing even if this means risking their own job or even personal security.

The mindset here is typified by whistleblowers who want to do the right thing as they see it, regardless of the ramifications they bring on themselves.

I have read recently an article in *The Independent*, "What Makes A Whistleblower?" by Charlie Cooper, who interviewed five whistleblowers to find out why they did it. He states:

> What they all had in common was an early memory, or an early inspiration, that had burned into their consciousness and made them persevere against a higher power, knowing in their heart they were in the right, even as the walls closed in around them.

Drawing on our higher wisdom

How do we know what is "right" or "wrong?" Often there is no clear answer as the world becomes even more interconnected: one group may lose out as another group benefits. It's hard to please all. However. the Conscious Leader will have an ability to connect to their higher self or inner voice of wisdom.

There are many different explanations (some religious, some spiritual, some psychological) to explain our ability as humans to move into a quiet zone and focus our attention on a higher level of consciousness and draw comfort and answers from this consciousness. I write as if we are separated from it. However, it is my belief that this is simply another type of consciousness that we can tap into through our minds and bodies.

A Conscious Leader will hold the same belief – that we all have an ability to connect to a deeper source of wisdom, one that can give us 'right' answers in a moment of leadership where we need clarity and greater truth before we make a decision.

When we tap into this level of consciousness, typically there is a sense of oneness, a sense that this consciousness is the amalgamation of all consciousness. There is also a sense that a question asked in connection to this universal consciousness will give us the ultimate "big picture." The answer from this place of knowing is unlikely to take sides as there is no observation of duality.

In our usual level of consciousness, we exist in a world full of duality; it is one thing or another, day or night, black or white. Often leaders get caught up in this duality as groups hold seemingly opposite views (e.g., left- or right-wing politics). At the higher levels of consciousness, though, all truth can exist simultaneously, and we are simply looking for balance in the natural system.

What would it be like if the leaders of a company spent time in the Board Meeting asking themselves:

"What is this business' core purpose in the world?"

"How can we serve our customers better? Do we know what they really want?"

"What level of consciousness is our organisation in right now?"

"Who is operating from a high level of consciousness in our organisation? Can we get them to tell us their vision for the business in the next board meeting?"

"What would it be like if we knew that we were respected and valued by our team including the leader and could do and say whatever we thought was best for the organisation as a whole?"

"What would it be like if we then had a respectful, open and honest debate where we were all aiming for the best for the organisation?"

Everything needs balance

Everything in the natural world requires balance.

> If gravity is the glue that holds the universe together, balance is the key that unlocks its secrets. Balance applies to our body, mind and emotions, to all levels of our being. It reminds us that anything we do, we can overdo or underdo, and that if

the pendulum of our lives or habits swings too far to one side,
it will inevitably swing to the other.
                                          -Dan Millman 'The Laws of Spirit'

As we need balance, so do ecosystems, societies and business organisations. Conscious Leaders understand this and will consider all parts of a system before trying to ensure it is balanced. Conscious Leaders will not only seek balance in themselves and their lives, they will want a balance of different types of people and energies in their top team and across their organisations.

As the Leaders in the Western world have been picked from a small section of society, it is natural that the lack of balance in this system has led to a lack of balance in the results the system produces. There is another shift going on in the West – that of re-balancing the energy.

In Chinese medicine, there is the concept of yin and yang energy. Yang represents male energy and Yin represents female energy. However, the two different types of energies exist in each of us and need to be balanced for good health. This same principle can be applied to sound leadership.

With the recent challenges of the banking industry, people have been asking, "What went wrong and how?" Some of the answers have indicated that the attitude and behaviour of those in the banking industry were aggressive, greedy and short-sighted.

These traits have been attributed to men, as women are seen to be more collaborative, cautious and take a longer-term view. "Now is the time," the newspapers shout, "for women to play a greater role in the industry." This basic explanation is predicated on the stereotype that our society creates of men and women, but doesn't account for the fact that men can also be collaborative, cautious and take a longer-term view. There are plenty of examples of aggressive, greedy women who take a short-term view of life.

Our business world has traditionally promoted people who put themselves forward – i.e., ambitious people who speak up about their talents and how they expect to be promoted. Leaders in business may have missed the value of the quieter, less ambitious, collaborative, more risk-averse person who takes a long-term view.

The way we bring up our children – in a society that believes that women have certain personality traits and men have others – means that we condition boys and girls to comply with only showing the traits that are associated with their gender. This leads to leaders (both men and women) having an imbalanced way of behaving. There is too much yin or too much yang, and therefore, there are fewer options for the leader to choose from when reacting to a situation.

My work is to add more options for the leader to take, and this involves them drawing on both their innate yin and their innate yang energy.

As a Conscious Leader, you will have a wide range of ways of being from direct and stern to open and compassionate. This allows you greater flexibility and adaptability than your counterparts who may still be playing out the fixed model of behaviour that their socialisation gave them.

As a Conscious Leader, you will look to your own thoughts and energy, your team's predominant energetic state and your organisation's energy and realise where there is a lack of balance. You will have an awareness of the imbalance in your teams and your organisation because you are balanced.

Chapter Summary

At the end of this chapter, hopefully you have:
- Tried on an abundance mentality and seen how this could affect your organisation
- Thought about your organisation's vision and purpose in the world and connected to how your role is helping your customers/clients/the environment, etc.

- Got some personal experience throughout this book so far of connecting to your own "inner wisdom" or "higher self" and understand the huge benefits this can bring you throughout your career
- An understanding of the concept of balance in Leadership – balance of energy types (yin and yang) within yourself, within your team and across whole societies when making decisions about how to do business and how to create the world we live in.

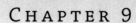

CHAPTER 9

Understand What You Need To Do To Get Results

Introduction

In this Chapter, I discuss the modern role of the Conscious Leader:
- What Conscious Leaders chose to spend their days doing
- How Conscious Leaders chose to spend their days BEING and how this is more important to focus on than simply WHAT TO DO
- A blue print for being a successful Conscious Leader

Often, my clients are in the process of shifting from a person who actually did the work and created results for their organisation to a leader of those who actually do the work. Even at CEO level, clients will often ask:

"So what am I supposed to do all day, if I empower everyone else to achieve the results for me?"

In a nutshell, the role of a leader is to keep the energy field productive, to facilitate a meaningful vision/purpose and keep everyone on track to get there. I explain more fully what an energy field is and how they are made in Chapters 10.

There are, of course, many other things that leaders need to do. The three categories below simply highlight the top level.

1) To truly **facilitate** others to come up with a joint vision that feels worth going for (a vision with purpose) – not creating the vision yourself. How to facilitate is discussed in more detail in Chapter 13.
2) To insist on rigourous and disciplined thinking, creating measureable goals and a clear path of action towards the vision.
3) To maintain momentum, once everyone is on track, by supporting those who need to do the work – also deciding when to amend the goals and planning to adjust to reality along the way.

In my book *Creating High Performing Teams*, I set out some practical exercises that leaders can run with their teams to help gain a joint vision and create SMART Goals and a clear plan to deliver the vision.

In this book, I focus much more on the skill of facilitation (in Chapter 13) and explaining how you can maintain you STATE to effectively carry out the third role above.

I liken the third role of a leader to the sport of curling. This sport entails players sliding polished granite stones across a sheet of ice towards a circular target on the ice. Once the stone has been launched on its path, there is automatic momentum, but the irregularities on the surface of the ice could throw the stone off target or slow it down so much that it doesn't reach the target. Then members of the curling team run in front of the stone and sweep the surface of the ice in the stone's path to aid it hitting its mark.

Setting the vision, goals and plan is like setting the target on the ice that the curlers must hit. The Conscious Leader's role then in step 3 (above) is to sweep the surface of the ice to allow the organisation to hit its target.

Throughout these three basic roles, the leader is required to manage their own emotional state because all around them people will sometimes be feeling stressed or overwhelmed.

It is at this point that the leader needs to be aware of how others are feeling and help bring their people back to a calmer place where clear solutions and good decisions can take place.

This role involves being constantly tuned into the emotional field around you so that you can deliberately intervene if the field becomes contaminated by people's anxiety and frustration. The role of a Conscious Leader is to pick up on the change in the emotional field. This is done by the leader being highly aware of how they are feeling, as well as realizing that they are being contaminated by the energy in the emotional field.

So if I feel anxious, I can stop and ask myself (a) "Is this my own anxiety that I'm creating with my thoughts, and if so what are the thoughts that I'm running? Or (b) "Am I picking up the anxiety in the room/organisation that is generated by those around me?"

If the answer is (a), I then need to consciously decide if I want to keep these thoughts or if I can focus my mind on another truth. If the answer is (b), then I need to consciously shift my own state to one of calm in order to influence the emotional field back to one of calm. This ability is one of the most fundamental skills a leader needs to have. Some call this resilience. It is also an area of leadership development that is only recently being taught.

To train leaders in a particular skill, it's important to be able to separate out that skill and identify it clearly. I have tried to do this at a basic level below.

It's HOW you are BEING that counts, not just WHAT you are DOING.

HOW you are BEING as a leader on a day-to-day basis is vital to your success. We have all probably experienced DOING something like hanging curtains, or fixing something, handling children or animals, when we have been in a state of frustration or in a hurry-up mode (HOW BEING).

We know that the results we get when we are in this state of being are far worse than the results we get when we are DOING any of these things in a state of calm (HOW BEING). This is the same for leaders dealing with all the things that they do in a day.

As a leadership coach, my clients tend to know what they should be doing (even if that is deciding to speak to an expert, a mentor, or their own team to decide what to do). My role, as their coach, is much more focused on how they are BEING, before they then decide WHAT to do.

Restructure		Consciously aware of it
New processes	**WHAT DO**	Written/Spoke about
Re-finance		Measurable
Frustrated		Not consciously aware
In a hurry	**HOW BEING**	Unwritten/Not discussed
Passionate		Unmeasurable

Traditional leadership training has been focused on the WHAT DOING. This is probably because it's far easier to train people on what to do than it is to help people develop HOW they are BEING.

The key is to consciously choose which state you want to be in for each task. The first step is to make the HOW BEING more conscious, so you are more aware of your own state of being as well as those around you.

Chapter Summary

This chapter has covered the key areas that Conscious Leaders need to focus on. Now you should have an understanding that as a Conscious Leader, you will be spending a lot of your time asking yourself, "What state am I in right now, and therefore, how am I BEING?"

You will not be focused on what you are DOING because you will have delegated the actual work to your team.

CHAPTER 10

Consciously Influence The Energetic Field

Introduction

Chapter 4 looked at how our THOUGHTS lead to our STATE.

Chapter 5 explained that when we are with another person, it is the state that we hold that is picked up by them as opposed to the actual words and actions that we are doing.

Human beings are social animals, and without language, we can still communicate a great deal of basic information: does this person like me? Are they angry with something or with me? Are they scared? Are they likely to be 'safe' to be with or 'unsafe' to be with?

Following on from these concepts, this chapter discusses:
- How a group of humans together generate an energetic field
- How if someone strongly holds a STATE then others unconsciously get "contaminated" by this state and their state shifts to become the same

- Because you are consciously aware of your own STATE – i.e., the type of energy that you are emitting you can change this and therefore change the energetic field
- THE SINGLE BIGGEST FACTOR FOR SUCCESS for all organisations

States are contagious.

Have you ever been to a concert and felt the energy of thousands of people all in a state of excitement and joy? The energy generated through excitement and joy is much higher and more powerful than if you were the only member of the audience watching the performance on your own.

That is because emotional states are contagious! If I meet you and 93% of my communication is the state that I'm in, then you must be able to feel in your body similar feelings to mine. This is how you pick up what I'm feeling.

When we see another person displaying a state of fear, we put ourselves in their shoes and can feel fear too. This is how suspense films work. The audience is literally tricking their bodies by imagining that they are in the same environment and situation as the actor in the film (step 1). They begin to run the same types of thoughts/meanings about their environment (step 2), and so their bodies automatically shift to a state (step 3) that is generated by these thoughts.

We do a similar thing with everyone around us. Some people do this more than others, and they have practiced (normally unconsciously) over years picking up other people's emotional states. These people have a high Emotional Intelligence (EI). Others that haven't had a path that led them to do this so much are deemed to have a lower EI. However, it is just that they are not in the habit of picking up other people's emotions.

The ability to do this is incredibly useful for leaders. I believe most people can be trained to raise their EI. Those who simply cannot pick up how others feel are deemed psychopathic. This is a very low percentage of the population.

So, as we are designed to pick up the emotions of those around us, it means that emotions can become contagious. If you are surrounded by anger and fear then you will unconsciously become angry or fearful too, even if you don't know why others are in this STATE! In a mass of people who are laughing and are joyful, it's difficult not to smile and laugh, too, even if you don't know what the joke is!

How does knowing this help leaders?

Once you understand that the state you are in is contagious, then being aware of your own state and consciously managing it becomes even more important.

What energy do you want your organisation to be operating from: fear/anger or confident/excitement?

Similarly, it also means that, as a leader, if you hold a calm, centered state for long enough and strongly enough, acting always from this place, then you will be able to consciously shift everyone else's states.

This is the hero in the film who stands still and silent, whilst everyone else in the room is shouting and angry. Slowly, the other people in the room pick up the hero's energy and unconsciously shift their own to match his/her state. The room slowly becomes quiet. (There is always the last one in the room who is the least emotionally intelligent who finds himself/herself shouting into silence and looks around to see the hero standing silently, calmly.) And only then does the hero speak. It is their strength of state that has shifted the whole room.

In many ways, it seems that Gandhi managed to do this amongst the hysteria and bloodthirsty cries of the British and Indian people.

We know that this is truly powerful leadership. We're getting into the realm of heroes and legends; however, this is something that we are all capable of doing. More importantly, this is something I believe can be learned. It is something that is most required in our leaders.

One of the key areas of training that I focus on with the leaders that I work with is firstly to be aware of and then able to manage their own energy field and then to practice in a safe environment, consciously shifting the group energy field. In this state of awareness, the leader can also think clearly and strategically. This moment of clarity may save an organisation from collapse!

Leaders who spend time in their clear thinking state, while all those around them are in a state of agitation or anger and blame, are hugely respected. They allow the rest of their people to shift into clear thinking states, too. When people are in a state of panic, anger, depression, they are not so productive as when they are acting from a state of calm, and level headed thinking.

In this way, the leader manages to fully mobilize their people right at the time when the organisation most needs productivity and clear strategic thinking.

Thoughts create reality

Groups of people working together on multiple projects that all add up to shifting their organisation forward is a highly complex thing. We have generated huge numbers of models, processes, theories and thus consultants to help organisations manage this complexity and to help leaders "make it work."

What if we had just not realized that WHAT YOU DO is not as important a factor of success as HOW YOU ARE BEING when you do it?

Currently, organisations are trying to improve their performance and profit base by changing:

- the structure
- the people
- their roles and job titles
- how their performance is measured
- the leader
- the brand and marketing material, etc.

Does this sound familiar? How many of these changes have occurred in your organisation in the last couple of years?

We as individuals also try and improve our own performance and happiness by changing our:

- organisation
- role
- place of work
- home
- hobbies
- partners
- bodies (from new hairdo to plastic surgery)
- cars, etc.

BUT people have not realized that all of that stuff is just like rearranging the deckchairs on the Titanic! The real way to improve performance, and therefore profit, for an organization is to shift the energetic field of that organization from one of anger, fear, tiredness and/or disconnectedness to connected, committed, excited, confident and creative.

How do we do that? We change our THOUGHTS, which then change our STATE. Our STATE is then transmitted to everyone around us and we change the ENERGETIC FIELD. If we are leaders, we have even more power to change the energetic field because in a hierarchy those below you are even more motivated to unconsciously connect to your STATE and adjust their state to match yours.

The real way to improve our own performance, and therefore our own sense of satisfaction with ourselves and our lives, is to shift our own energetic field.

Creating energetic fields

This phenomenon in which humans transmit their emotional state to others – and therefore others are "contaminated" by the same emotion – is one that I call 'creating energetic fields.'

It's like each person is walking around with an energy field emanating from him/her. If we could see and touch these fields of energy, they may look like a circle of coloured light around the person.

As people group together, they create one large energy field with the most dominant state becoming the common energy. This is how mob energy forms and rioting can break out. There is a strong sense of the energy of anger and fear when you come close to the mob.

The larger the number of people all contributing to the energy field, the more powerful the field becomes. It is obvious that 100,000 people all chanting together in the street is more powerful than just 10 people.

Where there is a large group of people gathering together (e.g., a football stadium, a religious ceremony, a state funeral, a dance festival), there is capacity to generate a powerful energy field that can almost overwhelm the individual.

If you are a leader who is consciously aware of your own emotional shifts and can be really present during meetings, then you don't need to ask people how they feel, you will feel it automatically. Not only that, but you can consciously change the energy field.

Anyone can do this. We all know someone who brightens up a room as soon as they walk in. We all know people who have the opposite effect, and we leave their company feeling tired and disconcerted.

How to become the storyteller

We all tell ourselves the story of our lives – i.e., what has happened to us and why. We re-run these stories, and they are what make us who we are. In reality, though, the past has gone, it is only our THOUGHTS and therefore STATE about it that remains. We could consciously re-create our past – not by saying that things never happened (that is simply denial), but by shifting how we view it, shifting the perspective from where we view it, and therefore changing the meaning we give to it (our THOUGHTS about it).

A lot of my early work with leaders includes exercises that allow the leader to shift their story about something. In a similar way, the leader of an organisation is the chief storyteller. They have the most power to decide how to reflect on the past and what it means to the organisation. They are also the most powerful person to influence the journey that the organisation is actually going through in real time.

As a Conscious Leader, you would plot the emotional journey that your organisation (or parts of your organisation) are on. Where are they now? What are they feeling, and what thoughts are they running to make themselves feel like that? These are they types of questions you would be asking yourself.

You would then look at the story of your organisation including its potential, where it could go and what you could do. This level of connection and recognition to what has come before and then the positive beliefs of what the current people in this organisation already have and the positive beliefs of what you could all achieve to help your customers/the world in some way. This is inspirational leadership.

Courage to feel all states

You cannot lead anyone from their current STATE until you have first identified with that state yourself – e.g., if you can't stand to feel despondent and down yourself, then you will be unable to shift a group of despondent and down people. You will avoid feeling this state yourself and therefore never connect with these people. They will pick up on the fact that you fear this state, or that it makes you annoyed to see people in this state (because you fear it). They will unconsciously know that you are not one of them, don't understand them and will not completely trust you to lead them.

In Chapter 6, I discuss the need to be able to accept all of the emotions that humans can feel. That is because for a Conscious Leader to influence the energetic field, you must be able to identify with it in yourself first. You can then start to identify the thoughts that you can run instead that will bring you out of this state and into a more productive state and eventually by holding this state strongly, others will become contaminated by it and you will have consciously changed the energetic field.

NOTE: This is no easy thing! If all leaders could do this, there would be no need to spend millions on cultural change programmes or go through all of the external processes, structural changes, etc. that are bullet pointed above.

Fortunately, the ability to consciously manage the energetic field back to a positive and productive state is the single biggest factor that will increase the success of an organisation!

YES, A HUGE STATEMENT!

However, now you are aware of how humans work, how we create energy fields (nearly always unconsciously) and how an organisation, whatever it is doing, is just made up of humans working together.

If you ran an organisation that could not yet afford operational infrastructure, such as office space, desks, phones, IT systems, or employing people to manage your finances, then getting these things in place would have a bigger impact than influencing the energetic field.

However, in the business world, where every organisation already has the basic operational infrastructure, then the only way to become successful is through the people. Not just who you recruit – their skills, knowledge and experience – but really:

- the amount of energy, focus and creativity each person gives each day
- the way they work together (internal efficiencies as well as emotional support)
- the energetic field that they are emitting to the world as a group (which is then picked up by any other person who interacts with the organisation)

Chapter Summary

This chapter reveals:

- the concept of energetic fields and that we are already operating unconsciously in a multitude of different energetic fields
- how, as a leader, to consciously change the energetic field
- some of the ramifications of being able to change the energetic field
- what I believe to be THE SINGLE BIGGEST FACTOR OF SUCCESS for all organisations.

In the next chapter, I elaborate on the ramifications of an organisation creating a positive energetic field.

CHAPTER 11

The Five Big Benefits for An Organization

Introduction:

The five big benefits for any organisation operating from a higher level of consciousness (i.e., with leaders who are operating from a higher level of consciousness and a subsequent culture that encourages all employees to operate from this high level of consciousness) are:

1) Attraction of more clients/customers
2) Attraction of more/better investors/shareholders
3) Creation of innovative, highly productive cultures
4) Attraction of top talent
5) Attraction of new opportunities

Leaders have the biggest effect on the energy field of their organisation because they directly affect the way everyone else in that organisation operates. I will explain in separate paragraphs below, how each one of the five benefits materializes.

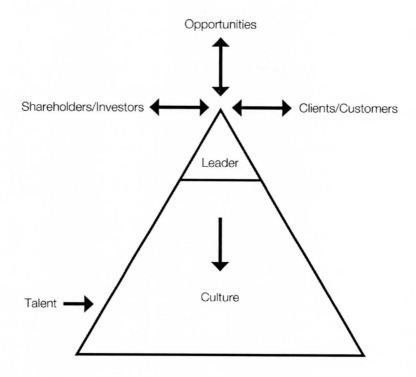

1) More clients/customers

In a similar way, to attracting top talent, an organisation that is generating a positive energy field will attract more customers and clients, or the best customers and clients (i.e., the ones that have the most choice).

The organisation's true brand will be known in the marketplace. This is not the brand that the organisation decides it wants to portray to the public, but the actual reality of its values that will be reflected outwards into the world. True branding can only be aligned with new true inner culture. It is like a person that we first meet and only see the image that they want to portray, but sooner or later through more interactions with them, we pick up clues as to their real thoughts about themselves. Then we realize that in order to have maintained such a different (and positive) image to the world, they must actually feel quite insecure about who they truly are.

An organisation's image to the world works in the same way. Those organisations that are happy with who they are, how they work and what they stand for are secure enough to have true branding. In fact, they are enlightened enough to look inside their company first and ask who they really are and spend time, effort and money, making their brand reflect this. Often, my work involves helping companies shift their true inner way of being first, so that they can genuinely live up to their brand aspirations.

2) More investors/shareholders

An organisation led by a consciously developed leader, who generates a positive energy field, will also attract investors because the organisation will be flourishing and showing confidence in the future, with lots of energy and ideas.

In the marketplace, such an organisation will be being talked about as a "mover and shaker" because of its innovative and creative way of being. Or it will be said to be a "hot ticket" because everyone is drawn to its positive field.

We instinctively know just by walking into an organisation's offices, or by meeting a group of its representatives, that the organisation feels like it's going places.

Investors are unconsciously tapping into the energy field of an organisation through their own bodies. Yes, they will obviously look at the numbers and analyze the validity of the market for its organisation's products and services. But there is no substitute for sitting in a board meeting and picking up the dynamics between the leaders. There is no substitute for walking around an organisation's offices to getting a sense of how it feels to work there.

Which investor wouldn't want to stake their money on the success of an organisation where the majority of people working for that organisation are thinking "We have great Leaders and staff, there is an abundance of opportunity for us right now, and we are positioned to provide great value to the market place with our innovative products and services, so we're excited and proud to be part of this?"

3) Innovative, productive culture

If there is a positive energy field created by the top team, this gets transmitted throughout the organisation, creating a culture of positive energy. If you spend a day in this type of organization, you will feel energized by the people around you. There will be an energy field of focused, high productivity in a calm, centered way as well as passion, drive and excitement.

There would be a sense of ownership and the ability to feel safe to own up to mistakes because the enlightened Leader will have accepted their own faults and know that we all make mistakes -- especially when we are learning something new or breaking new ground, which are two things which the leader wants everyone to be doing anyway.

A consciously developed leader is also coming from a mindset of shifting paradigms. They have the ability to "think outside the box." In Rooke and Torbert's Model of Leadership Development, those at level 6 generate transformational change in organziations and people. How? They "exercise the power of mutual inquiry, vigilance, and vulnerability for both the short and long term." This must lead to higher levels of innovation and creativity, not just in the leader's mind but in the culture that they create.

Ikujiro Nonaka is professor of management at the Institute for Business Research of Hitotsubashi University in Tokyo, Japan. He pointed out that the serendipitous quality of innovation was highly recognized by managers and linked the success of Japanese enterprises to their ability to create knowledge not by processing information but rather by "tapping the tacit and often highly subjective insights, intuitions, and hunches of individual employees and making those insights available for testing and use by the company as a whole."

Harvard Business Review. 1991, p. 94. November–December issue.

Further, Napolean Hill stated:

> Through the faculty of creative imagination, the finite mind of humankind has direct communication with Infinite Intelligence. It is the faculty through which 'hunches' and 'inspirations' are received. It is by this faculty that all basic or new ideas are developed. It is through this faculty that thought vibrations from the minds of others are received.
> - *Think And Grow Rich*, 1937

What Napolean Hill calls "infinite intelligence," I call "universal consciousness," but I think we are talking about the same phenomenon.

4) Attract talent

An organisation that is generating such a huge positive energy field will be able to attract the best talent in the market. Not only will their organisation have a reputation for being a positive, exciting and developmental place to work, when potential employees come into contact in any way with the organisation through the recruitment process, they will experience this positivity.

We are naturally, often unconsciously, drawn to positivity. We all want to live and work in an environment that fosters growth. Some organisations that I know today with this positive energy field not only attract the top talent, but pay them less than their competitors because whatever people say, they tend to be more motivated by career opportunities and personal development in a fun, safe environment, than by money.

5) Attract new opportunities

It seems that the leaders, teams and organisations which are generating positive fields of energy and constantly thinking in a consciously developed way, appear to attract opportunity.

These opportunities may or may not be taken up, but they seem to appear from nowhere. I am not talking about a potential client who decides to chose your organization; I'm talking about an opportunity of which you had no conscious awareness until it is presented to you as an opportunity almost out of the blue.

We often talk about "coincidences" or things that were "just lucky," and it does seem that those leaders and organisations that create positive fields of energy are "lucky."

I have often had clients who have become consciously aware of their own path. They realize that they have something specific to contribute through their career and that they are already on this path, but they had just not been aware of it until now. They have faith that each step feels right and somehow they will realize their vision. Holding this conscious state of faith and a clear vision seems to allow them to be open to seemingly lucky coincidences.

One client described to me the exact type of person they needed to meet in order to take their business to the next level. They felt that somehow their paths would cross, and they would simply have faith in that and keep their eyes peeled for this type of person. Within a week they called me, very excitedly, to tell me that they had literally bumped into one of these people in a lift, got chatting, then realized what a coincidence that was!

If your organisation is emanating a positive energy, the type of opportunities you will attract will be with equally positive people/ organisations. If however the organisation is emanating negative energy of greed or fear, then those they attract to partner will be equally emanating a state of greed or fear. Like attracts like. This goes for all types of relationships, not just business relationships.

We feel safe to trust people like us, so if we are operating from a high level of consciousness, we will choose to do business with people operating from this same level of consciousness. It also means that if a business is still operating from levels 1 - 3 in Richard Barrett's model, then they are operating from fear of not getting what they need (e.g., money, status, power). They will also choose, unconsciously, to do business with people and organisations that are also operating from this fear base of ego and need.

Chapter Summary

So by now, hopefully you will understand why being aware and being able to change the energetic field is the SINGLE BIGGEST FACTOR OF SUCCESS for all organizations that already have the physical infrastructure required to operate a business – e.g., office space, desks, phones, IT systems, etc.

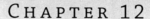

CHAPTER 12

Solve All Problems Through Change of Thought

Introduction

In this chapter, I also make a very bold statement! All problems can be solved if we change what we think about the problem. It is only our thoughts about life, the world, ourselves, our capabilities, our separateness, etc. that caused the problem in the first place!
I also discuss:

- how if you think of something negative, you will experience the world negatively and vice versa
- how if you want to create something that is not yet in the world, you need to imagine it in your thoughts first

It's what you think that counts.

Intrinsically, we know that it's what someone thinks that is most important. We care about people's beliefs, when someone tells us what they think about something, and when we don't think the same, we are hugely affected and we put a lot of effort into trying to get them to think like us. Why? Because we know that everything comes from thought. We are all continuously creating – not just our subjective reality, but the actual reality in our outer world based on our initial thought.

Unconsciously creating

Most of the time, we are creating reality unconsciously and just pointing to the problem in the outer world, not understanding our part in it. If I am conditioned to believe that I'm not very clever, then I won't try hard at school, so I won't get good grades, hence the proof that I'm not very clever in the outer world. Everyone around me will also treat me as if I am not very clever, so the outer world reinforces my initial belief.

Rosenthal was a distinguished Professor of Psychology at the University of California, Riverside. Lenore F Jacobson was principal of an elementary school in the South San Francisco Unified School District in 1963. They began corresponding and eventually ran an experiment with teachers and pupils to see if the teacher's expectations (thoughts) of their pupils had an effect on the actual performance of those pupils.

School children were selected at random by the researchers, so that each class had children with a range of abilities. The teachers, however, were told that one class was full of high potential students but the other was not. Rosenthal and Jacobsen found that these expectations created their own reality. The teachers' expectations influenced their behaviors towards the two different classes of children, which in turn influenced the children's performance. So, the false expectations caused the teachers to genuinely experience one class as being full of bright students and the other as not.

Because the teachers held these beliefs about their group of children, the children actually performed to those expectations. The children that were in the "bright student" class performed to a higher standard than the children that were not. This self-fulfilling prophecy was defined as the process by which a perceiver's (the teacher) expectations about a person (the child) eventually lead that child to confirm those expectations.

This has a profound impact on business, talent management and knowing what the leaders of organisations are thinking about their staff. Have you ever experienced a decrease or increase in your performance based on what another person has thought about your abilities to perform? Have you ever started a new job, full of excitement and confidence, only to find after 6 months, that you are starting to make mistakes? You start to think, "I'm not as good as I thought I was" or "How did I get to be so bad, I used to think I could do this well?"

Unfortunately, this lowering of performance is a more common experience than the experience of being so encouraged, trusted, and managed well that our performance increases. Hopefully you have some of these referential experiences, too.

Consciously creating

We can choose to consciously create something new in the outside world by first visioning it, thinking about what it would be like and using our imagination. This thought may come from a perceived problem in the outer world that we want to change. Martin Luther King's "I have a dream" is a good example of this use of creating a dream future in his imagination that he then shared with others, so that they could also see how the future could be. Or it may simply come from wanting to create something that has never been created before because that brings us intrinsic joy that we want to share with others.

The concept that we create reality in the world by first creating a thought, then the word and then the deed, is not new. In fact, there are references to this in most religious texts. The key message in Napolean Hill's famous book *Think And Grow Rich*, is the fact that we can create reality from our thoughts.

How unconsciously we experience reality

Depending on the habitual thoughts that we rehearse, we will create a world that reflects back to us our own beliefs. We will track for what we believe in, decide to focus on only the things we feel are important and experience only our subjective reality.

It is like two people that go to the same party. At the end of the night, one says "That was a great party. I spoke to lots of new interesting people and had a laugh." The other may say, "That was a terrible party. The drinks were warm, and I didn't like the music." They both have a self-created reality. No two people can experience the same reality.

It's important to realize that it's our own thoughts that are creating our reality. It's how we interpret and react to our environment that creates our reality, not the actual external environment.

What does this mean for leaders?

We are often not aware that it is our own thoughts that are making us act in a certain way. We aren't aware that how we habitually act is transmitted to the world, and the world will then reflect back to us the perceived reality that we've created in our own heads.

> In a classic study by researchers Betty Grayson and Morris I Stein, Stein asked convicted criminals to view a video of pedestrians walking down a busy New York City sidewalk, unaware they were being taped. The convicts had been to prison for violent offences such as armed robbery, rape, and murder. Grayson and Stein asked the convicted criminals to let them know if there was anyone in the video that they would target.
>
> Within just a few seconds, the convicts identified which pedestrians they would have been likely to target. What startled the researchers was that there was a clear consensus among the criminals about whom they would have picked as victims—and their choices were not based on gender, race, or

age. Some petite, physically slight women were not selected as potential victims, while some large men were.

The researchers realized the criminals were assessing the ease with which they could overpower the targets based on several nonverbal signals—posture, body language, pace of walking, length of stride, and awareness of environment. Neither criminals nor victims were consciously aware of these clues.

-Chuck Hustmyre, Jay Dixit,
Psychology Today, January 2009

So if your experiences in life are feeding back some commonality – e.g., I have had my bag stolen three times, or I have been turned down for promotion twice in the same company – then take some time to connect to yourself and your deep wisdom and see if there are any unconscious beliefs you are running that are being transmitted to the external world and reflected back in your reality.

Exercise – Thoughts create reality

1) Think of something you would like to do better, or something you don't do but would like to do.
2) When you think of doing this thing, notice how you feel in your body. Write this down.
3) Now go back to imagining doing this thing, feel what state you are in and notice what thoughts you have about this activity, about yourself, others and anything else that comes to mind. Write down the exact sentences that you are saying to yourself in your head. Put quotation marks around these sentences to show that this is the unconscious "script" you are running.
4) Turn to a new page in your notebook. Think about something you love to do and do well.
5) Notice how you feel when you think of this. Write it down.
6) Notice what you think about this activity yourself, others, etc. Write this down and put quotation marks around the entire sentences you are saying to yourself.

7) Now compare the two processes you are running for the first action and for the activity you love to do. Can you see that your thoughts and state are the things that are determining your reality?

8) Make a list of the new, more positive (but equally true) thoughts that you could chose to run through your mind for the action you want to do better.

9) When you read these thoughts, how do you feel now?

10) What does this state allow you to do in the world now?

You have consciously changed your reality. If you continue to run these new thoughts through your mind, you will feel this new state and take these new actions in the world. You will also change your reality because you will eventually become better, even great, at doing this new activity and the better you become, the more you will enjoy it. You will create a positive feedback loop between THOUGHT, STATE, ACTION in the diagram in Chapter 4, without having to change the TRIGGER (the outside world).

Consciously turning around the problems in the outer world

Realising your power

Any problem you have in your own life or in your business world will simply be a reflection of your own thoughts, state and actions in response to that problem. The outer world is simply the environment. It can be extremely challenging for us to have to adjust to our environment so that we don't suffer so many problems. (Although I believe that it's the human experience to have problems to overcome, it's this that allows us to grow and develop.)

So for any leader I'm coaching, I ask "what are your problems?" I want to know: what is happening in the outer world that you wish wasn't happening? Or what is not happening/being created that you have a desire to have happen/create?

It really doesn't matter what it is. Everything is a chance for us to become more consciously aware of what thoughts we are entertaining, what energy field we are generating and sending out into the world.

I am focused on two goals for my client:
1. The first goal is to help them set and reach their organisational goals.
2. The second goal is to help them raise their levels of consciousness through the process of achieving the first goal.

Obviously, once we take full responsibility for our own way of being in respect to a perceived problem, then we have total power to change that. It is really only ourselves that we can change but to wake up and realize how powerful we really are is normally awe-inspiring. This awakening or "light bulb moment" can also be followed by a sense of fear as we realize the enormous responsibility that comes with being Conscious Leaders.

How to use this power

If there are different realms, the realm of THOUGHT, (see the diagram in Chapter 4) the realm of STATE and the realm of ACTION, then we can start to determine how to solve problems as leaders. We can decide if this problem lies in the action realm, then what is the state that goes with that action, and therefore, what are the thoughts?

This logical thinking can help resolve almost any problem that a business faces in the outer world – the world where physical things happen and actions are taken as opposed to the inner world of thought and feeling.

Example

If your business needs more clients, but you are not winning any, my questions to you as the Leader would be these: "How do you feel about this? What are you thinking about this problem?" I know it's in the THOUGHT realm that I need you to shift. Once you can create alternative thoughts that could also be true and that generate a positive energized state, then I know that the actions you decide to take in the outer world will lead to you attracting more clients.

If you remain in a negative thought space, generating states of fear that unconsciously spreads to your team and the rest of your organisation, then you will create an even bigger problem in the outer world.

Case Study

I once worked with a team that kept telling me, "We just need a kick up the backside and to win more business." I asked them what state they felt they were in at that moment, and many were in a state of frustration and fear.

I explained that clients aren't going to want to be "contaminated" by that energy. That was their state that would be transmitted over the phone to potential clients, and instinctively, most people would move away from this state of frustration and fear.

They still didn't seem to grasp my theory, so I said, "Okay, who has ever been on a first date?" A show of hands went up. "When you went on this date were you thinking to yourself, 'There aren't many women in the world, so I'd better make sure I end up with this one; I really need to get this woman to meet me again because if she doesn't I will have failed and if I fail it will be because I'm not really that interesting a person?'"

They laughed and said, "That date wouldn't go so well. You'd come across as desperate."

"Yes," I replied, "that is exactly how you are coming across to your potential clients!"

They decided that they didn't want to be the "desperate dater team" as they called themselves. "Then let's get another identity," I suggested. They began to work on some alternative positive beliefs about their product, their organisation and how a client would benefit from signing up with them.

By the end of the session, one of them said, "Tou know what? I think we can really make these people's lives just a little bit easier. I don't feel like we have to sell anything to them. Just explain what we can offer them if they'd like it."

The tipping point

To reverse this thinking and state can take a huge conscious effort. Initially, leaders and top teams often need a lot of support to do it and keep going with it, but there is always a tipping point when things begin to turn around. It takes less conscious effort from the Leader because he/she has created a positive field, which in turn generates even more positivity and spreads out into the marketplace. In this day and age, with the use of the worldwide web, this energy can spread rapidly across the globe.

Example:

Why do we still have only 15% of female directors in the top 100 companies in the UK? This problem exists in the outer world, so we really want to ask the leaders and those in power, what do you truly think about women in the boardroom? Then, how does this make you feel? We also want to ask women what they truly think about being on the board and how this makes them feel.

I know that the outer reality of the world – e.g., not enough women at board level is only caused by the inner thoughts/beliefs of our collective society. Once these thoughts are fully understood, we can openly discuss them and ask, "Is that belief really serving us?" and consciously change it.

Once enough people in society hold different thoughts –such as thoughts and beliefs that will facilitate more women working at board level – then the outer world will reflect this, too, and more women will begin influencing how organisations are led by being fully valued members of the board or executive management team.

Until the THOUGHTS change, people's STATE won't change, and therefore, what they do or do *not* do (ACTION) won't change and society won't change. Their thoughts are creating the actual reality reflected in the outer world.

Of course, women are integral to society and form part of the whole fabric, so in this case, it is not simply changing the thoughts around the role of women as directors of organisations, but also the role of men and women about managing every other task required to have a healthy society – e.g., care of children, elderly, managing a household, etc.

Consciously Creating - The need for imagination

So far, we have discussed how we react to our environment. However, leaders also need to understand how to create reality using their imagination.

Everything you see that has been manmade or man-transformed (like our natural world) had to begin with a thought. In Napolean Hill's book *Think and Grow Rich*, he gives us a step-by-step guide to how to "grow rich." The first step is to think.

There is nothing we can do that we have not thought of first. The first step in creating anything new (e.g., globalizing the business, implementing a new IT system, obtaining a good team dynamic) is to imagine it first.

Where does our creativity come from? There are many discussions on this, however I will simply put forward the way I have seen people create and share my own beliefs on this topic.

First, connect to your five senses.

We need to connect to our five senses to connect to our environment and take in the universe. Every split second of the day we are taking in the universe, storing trillions of bits of data that are fed through our senses. Most of this data is filtered and stored, but we would be totally overwhelmed if it was all pushed to our conscious mind for us to make meaning of it.

There is an understanding that the unconscious mind stores every piece of data. All that raw understanding of the complex world we live in is stored somewhere, somehow.

As I have mentioned before, it's my belief that there is universal consciousness or universal wisdom – a sense that it's not just the trillions of bits of data that each of us individually store in our own unconscious mind, but also some form of group consciousness that we can also tap into. We still don't know where a thought comes from, how our imagination works or why one person is inspired to create one thing and another person is inspired to create another thing.

Martin Luther King called his vision "a dream," but what made him and not another person have this dream and have faith that it could be achieved, even through the challenges he faced?

Connect to your state of creativity

If you watch highly creative people at work, they first move consciously into a certain type of state. They experience this state differently, but it is a pleasant state to be in.

I believe we all experience this state of creativity and imagination when we are children, but we either get out of the habit of connecting to it or believe that we shouldn't waste our time in this "day dreaming" state.

By the time we are adults with demanding jobs, bills to pay and children to care for, we find that we spend hardly any time in our creative/imaginary state.

If someone's creativity was less tangible as a child, they may have grown into an adult believing that they just aren't "creative" at all. This is a tragedy, particularly in our leaders, because of the vital need for our leaders to think creatively, imagine a better future and inspire others to reach this vision.

Certainly, the ability to tap into our imagination is increased through practice, but we also need to be in a relaxed state physically, where we can let the mind wander and make new connections. If we are constantly in the active "to do" list state running thoughts like "I don't have time to do all of my to do list," then we certainly won't be as creative as we could be. The creative process is about surrendering the controlling conscious mind first and allowing ideas, pictures, feelings to come to you.

Have you ever experienced a time when you were trying to think of the name of someone/something and it's on the tip of your tongue, but the more your conscious mind tries to grasp it, the more illusive it becomes? Eventually, you say, "Oh, it will come to me later" and stop trying to think of it. Later, when you are relaxed in your body and your mind is also relaxed (not focused on any one thing), the answer comes to you. This is a bit like the creative process.

Current blocks to your creativity

In this modern age, leaders are often bombarded with information, emails to respond to, actions to do, etc. The biggest complaint I hear from leaders is "I don't have enough time to think" or 'If only I had more time, I could be more strategic.'

A shift in leadership to a place of creating your own reality, rather than reacting to the current status quo, is one of the single biggest success factors that Conscious Leaders do. Take charge of your time and know how to consciously move into a creative state in order to come up with a creative vision and strategy or creative solutions to problems.

Your daily practice – Takes 5 seconds

Conscious Leadership involves a daily practice – even if it is just one minute per day. This practice becomes as habitual as taking a daily shower. The practice is often referred to as "mindfulness," and the exercise in Chapter 6 can be cut down to a shortened version to run each day.

Simply taking a deep breath in, closing your eyes and noticing how you feel in your body right now is a start and only takes 5 seconds!

Chapter Summary

This chapter looks at:
- How problems are created – that there are only problems because of the beliefs/thoughts of all those involved in the problem.
- To solve a problem, you as the leader need to understand the thoughts of those who are part of creating the problem. At whole organization level, that will be everyone in the organization; at societal level, that will be everyone in society; at global level, that will be everyone in the world!
- How our thoughts are creating our subjective experience of reality, and therefore, when you are a Conscious Leader you can decide what experience you want to have in each moment of your lifetime.

- How anything that has ever been created in the world (unless it was an accident) has first been thought of in someone's imagination. As a Conscious Leader, you first need to be able to visualize the future of your organization before you can start to move towards it.

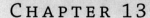

CHAPTER 13

Facilitate Group
To Make Good Decisions

Introduction

This chapter deals with one of the most fundamental, yet undervalued, skills for a Conscious Leader: true facilitation.

I also discuss:
- The need for facilitation
- Some key elements of facilitation
- One simple question to help maintain Conscious Leadership

Why do conscious leaders need to facilitate?

For many leaders, their role is to truly facilitate parties that seem to have opposing views. In order to get a joint vision of what the future could look like and an agreed plan, they need to first have the courage to make sure that all the parties that have an interest in this are in the room together and then facilitate, which is a separate skill in itself. Just getting the right people in the room can in itself be a huge task.

We live in a world of perceived duality, where there is left and right, day and night, right and wrong. However, to overcome the global challenges that leaders now face, we need to raise our levels of consciousness to be able to see that all these seemingly opposite truths can be true simultaneously.

At the board level within an organisation, the Conscious Leader will facilitate discussion around a key question that the organisation needs to answer – e.g., how do we continue to build our core capability as well as come up with new innovations? Every leader at any level will have questions that, if they knew the answers,, could improve the performance of the teams they lead.

If you as a Conscious Leader have developed and practiced the skills to truly facilitate these discussions, then you will be able to illicit the wisdom from all parts of the system –

i.e., hear everyone's different perspectives. At the board level, the HR Director will have a different perspective than the Finance Director who will have a different perspective than the IT Director and the Sales Director. This is because each person is unique, but also because each person only represents a part of the whole system. This is perfectly set up because you as the leader need to have the particular perspective of each different part of the system. To be able to encourage each voice, to hear each opinion without judgment and to understand where each person is coming from is vital BEFORE you weigh up all the opinions and make a decision.

Often each party will want to win. They will be trying to persuade you to go with just their way of thinking. However, the Conscious Leader knows that there does not need to be duality, there does not need to be "one way or the other." The Conscious Leader is looking to balance all the parts in the system. Looking to consider every voice in the boardroom (or even other representing voices within the organisation). A balanced way is likely to be successful; however, sometimes to side with a drastic option, which discounts the other options, is also the right thing to do. However, even if this is the case, the Conscious Leader will have chosen consciously! Each member of their team will know that they've had a chance to put forward their opinions and concerns; they know that they will have been heard and taken into considerations. When the Conscious Leader explains why they might have sided with just one part of the team (i.e., taken a direction that is not balanced between all parts), the rest of the team will understand why and hopefully back that decision as it will be the best decision for the whole.

As a Conscious Leader, you can hold uncertainty for a long time. You can be ok with not knowing the outcome of a discussion because you ultimately trust in the process of letting everyone speak, be heard and be valued.

If you as the Leader can hold this higher state of consciousness long enough for the room to be "contaminated" by your energy, others in the room can let go of their own individual ego-based view and move to a view based on what is best for the whole.

When groups of people provide a view based on what is best for the whole, those views may seem to be opposing, but they will all simply be representing a part of the system that needs to be considered and kept in balance. If you can make a decision, having considered all these disparate parts of the system, you will make a good decision.

If at least some of the group trust that you came prepared to have an open mind – that their views have been taken into consideration and you have heard everyone's view, then made a choice based on what is best for the whole – they will more likely respect your decision (even having seen that they would have come to the same decision themselves), and you will have buy-in from the group.

How to facilitate

When you facilitate, you must be clear about the role you are playing – and the role that you will NOT play. Often, an egotistical leader will take up most of the speaking time, they have already made up their minds about the decision and are simply playing to the audience, to try and persuade them to their view. They do hear the other people's views, but don't really consider them because they do not come with an open mind (ready for that mind to be persuaded by a series of different views); they have already made up their mind.

1) Manage your own state.

So a key first step is to be able to stay centered in your own state, when you do not know the answer. If you run thoughts like "I am the Leader, so I should know all the answers," then you will find it hard to stay in a calm state when you don't know the answers. You will probably avoid going into an anxious state by giving your answer too quickly. This closes down the open, creative energy field.

Be able to keep your center when you step into a group of people, who are all trying to persuade you to side with them. The THOUGHTS you could run here are:

- "I need to step in with no agenda, no outcome apart from to really stay present and listen"
- "These people deserve my respect as they are highly intelligent, know more about their areas than me and are just passionate about protecting/evolving the areas they are interested in."
- "My role is to model good listening, so that others will listen too."
- "I ultimately have control over the energetic field and can allow full passionate speaking, but I can also decide to slow everyone down anytime I feel that would be useful."

2) Allow full emotions, but then bring the energy field back to calm.

One of the roles that the you will play as a leader who is consciously facilitating the group is to keep everyone calm. You can do this by dropping in your own beliefs such as "We have plenty of time. It's important to listen to each person's point of view" and "If we hear everyone's worries about this, we can find a middle way and address the risks up front."

The key is to remain calm yourself. So often during highly charged facilitations, I have taken my focus from the external room of what everyone is saying and spent 10 seconds managing my own state to one of calm, compassion and gentle humour (because these are the energetic states that the field needs to become more balanced). Then I ACT –

i.e., stand up, slowly walk to the middle of the group, hold up my arm to gain attention, say "Okay, okay, okay, okay" in my tone of voice and facial expressions that are reflecting my genuine state (calm, compassionate, gentle humour).

I am consciously deciding to change the energetic field. I am using my ability to hold my own conscious state of calm, compassionate, gentle humour to "contaminate" the room, and unconsciously, everyone else begins to feel more of my state in themselves. Often, this allows for the group to laugh at themselves, take a breath, acknowledge that they are all passionate about this topic, but to start the discussions again from this connected base.

The results will be as good as the energetic field. If the energetic field is able to keep re-setting itself to calm, compassion, open, listening, etc. then the group will have a fruitful discussion, feel they have been heard and valued and when the time comes to make a decision, some (if not all) may already be operating from a mindset of "what is best for the whole" rather than "what is best for me/my team/my area."

3) Hold a big picture mindset.

When we are making decisions directly involving people, you as a Conscious Leader who is coming from a place of calm and deep wisdom may ask, "What is the most compassionate thing to do now? What is the best way forward for the whole? What can we do to mitigate the risks if we take this road?" You may also be asking yourself, "How does the energy field feel now? Is there someone who looks like they have more to say or is everyone aligned?"

One Simple Question to Help Maintain Conscious Leadership

In Chapter 9, I set out the three high level roles of the Conscious Leader. They were:

1) To facilitate the team to gain a vision that everyone can emotionally connect with.
2) To instill disciplined thinking so that the team can create SMART Goals from their vision and a clear plan of action
3) To maintain momentum, like the person sweeping the ice during a curling match.

To be a Conscious Leader, you not only need to become aware of the fact that (a) your THOUGHTS lead to your STATE and it is the quality of your STATE that forms the quality of your ACTIONS; you also need to (b) be constantly practicing this awareness and self management of your THOUGHTS and STATE because you know that it's HOW YOU ARE BEING that effects everything.

It is HOW YOU ARE BEING that is the difference between being a great leader and an average leader. It is HOW YOU ARE BEING that leads to teams and organisation gaining great results or average results.

So I have set out below, one simple question to keep asking yourself throughout the day – or if you are about to make a major decision:

"Am I doing this from a STATE of love (compassionate wisdom or joy), or a STATE of fear (or anger, jealousy etc?"

We often use the word "love" to say "I love my family, my car, that film, working on this project, feeling fit, etc." However, as leaders we don't often bring "love" into our workplace – at least not consciously.

It is not socially acceptable to ask a leader "Do you feel love when you are making this decision?" However, the ultimate test for doing the right thing in life is to act from love as opposed to fear.

Chapter Summary

At the end of this chapter, you should have a better idea of the following:

- The undervalued but essential role of the Conscious Leader is to truly facilitate.
- Some of the key THOUGHTS, therefore STATEs and therefore ACTIONS of a good facilitator are how to facilitate.
- How you can maintain Conscious Leadership throughout the day/week.

CHAPTER 14

Raise Levels of Consciousness In Others

Introduction

Once you are practicing Conscious Leadership, you will naturally be helping to raise the level of consciousness in others. As you continue to develop as a Conscious Leader, your ability to consciously say and do things to help others evolves. This chapter explains why this is and shows you how.

Stephen Covey's book *The 8th Habit* builds on his worldwide best seller, *The 7 Habits of Highly Effective People*. The 8th Habit is to "Find Your Voice and Inspire Others to Find Theirs":

> At the core, there is one simple, overarching reason why so many people remain unsatisfied in their work and why most organisations fail to draw out the greatest talent, ingenuity and creativity of their people and never become truly great, enduring organisations. It stems from an incomplete paradigm of who we are – our fundamental view of human nature.

> The fundamental reality is, human beings are not things needing to be motivated and controlled; they are four dimensional – body, mind, heart and spirit.

Covey goes on to show how if you develop your own voice and "walk your talk" you will be inspirational to others. If you actively encourage others to find their voice (their true path) and walk their talk, then you are making a huge contribution to the world. In Richard Barrett's model of levels of consciousness set out in Chapter 15, this is shifting from level 3 to level 4 and then helping others to shift from level 3 to level 4 - 7.

Becoming a mentor

There is a need for the cycle of leadership development to continue. Conscious Leaders will ultimately understand and accept the cycle of life. They know that nothing stays the same; the world and all of us in it are continually changing. They know that it is important to pass on their knowledge and skills to the next generation. They also feel that they would like to give back in some way. Perhaps they had some great guides and mentors on their journey, and at some point in their career, they would like to do the same for someone else.

Becoming a Coach

The Coaching industry and the integration of Neuro-linguistic Programming (NLP) in the business world has contributed to the general shifting to a higher level of consciousness. The shift is to the level where we start to let go of our conditioned beliefs, ego and fears and take courage to explore who we really uniquely are, what we want in our lives and what we can then give back.

By attending a good course in coaching, many leaders have had their own personal shifts and are on their way to reaching higher levels of consciousness. I believe that the skill of learning to become a good coach could be part of the way in which we fast track the developmental levels of leaders and all those around us.

The use of questions in coaching helps us to come to our own conclusions. We are not lectured to, or told what to think. Instead, we are asked to connect to our bodies, be still, close our eyes and then ask our inner voice of wisdom, "What is really important to me right now?" This helps us elicit our true core values and to follow our heart. By doing this, we will be able to find our own unique true identity and purpose.

Through the support of coaching, we can overcome our fears to break away from the herd and walk our path with courage. In Chapter 15, I set out some of the current models of levels of consciousness – the journey that we as human beings are all on. We can shift from levels 1-3 to level 4 in Richard Barrett's model; we can shift from level 4 to 5 in the Spiral Dynamics Model and from level 4 to 5 in Rooke and Torbert's Model. This initial shift then allows us to take further leaps.

The value of coaching

There are many examples of people who are operating from a higher level of consciousness. You may know of some around the world right now. There are many different versions of the role of assisting others to become more consciously aware and to operate from higher levels of consciousness. Being a coach is just one label for this role.

The level of consciousness that the coach has attained will have a huge affect on their level of coaching. The coach can only guide a client to the same level that they have attained. So I believe that our own personal development as coaches is what will allow us to best assist our clients solve their current business issues and achieve greater results for their organisations and for the world as a whole.

By living at your level of consciousness, you raise that of others.

Although there is still a debate amongst neurophysiologists, they have discovered specific neurons in the brain that have been called "mirror neurons." They believe these neurons are there to help us mirror or copy the behaviour of those around us. This is how, as children, we learn to speak with the same accent as our family, we learn to walk and then learn all of the socially acceptable and non-acceptable behaviours that our culture holds. We don't need to be told these things; we just start to copy the adults we spend a lot of time with.

Have you ever seen a child dressing up in their mother's clothes and walking around the house with an oversized handbag? Have you noticed how teenagers that hang out together pick up each other's ways of talking, walking, etc.? This continues to happen to us as adults. We can still heed our mother's warning to "choose friends wisely!"

This same phenomenon is occurring in the workplace, and this is how we form cultures. Anyone who meets you, works with you, or hears your opinion or way of doing things, will be unconsciously picking up your way of being. If they are operating from a lower level of consciousness, just by being connected to your thinking in some way will give them the chance to start to shift their own levels of consciousness.

This same phenomenon is how entire societies can move, for example, from the Dark Ages to the Renaissance. Which direction is a society moving in? We can measure this by looking at the amount of fear in society and by using the models set out in Chapter 15 to measure the level of consciousness of the majority of people within a culture.

It is when leaders connect to their "higher wisdom" and develop higher levels of consciousness that they are suddenly counterculture. Those that live and speak their truth, from a higher level of consciousness, know that they are risking the rejection of the masses. They may be heralded as the cutting edge thinkers of the day; however, they could equally be hounded, ostracised or ridiculed. It takes courage to stand up for what they believe because they know that it is not what most people are thinking and acting upon.

Chapter Summary

- By living from a higher level of consciousness, you will automatically help those around you raise their level of consciousness – unless they reject you in order to remain at their lower level.
- By actively mentoring and coaching others you will have evolved into a highly advanced Conscious Leader. This normally occurs in the later stages of a leader's career.
- One way to fast track leadership development is to train leaders to become mentors and coaches because to become successful in these roles, the leader must become a Conscious Leader operating from a high level of consciousness.

CHAPTER 15

The Map For Your Journey

Introduction

This chapter sets out the following models of levels of consciousness so that you can see the whole journey laid out before you (like a map) and identify where you are now and where you could develop to:

- Richard Barrett's Model of Human Consciousness
- Rooke and Torbert's model, "Seven Transformations of Leadership"
- Spiral Dynamics Model of Whole Society Transformation

Why do we need models/maps?

Without a map, we don't know where we are going – we may not even know where we are starting from!

With regard to your skill as a leader – i.e., your level of consciousness – I want to set out some of the current maps/models that show you the different levels of consciousness that you can attain.

If you like one or two of these models, you may wish to use them to continue measuring where your level of consciousness is in your life as a leader and how you have progressed over the coming years.

I would state now, though, that I don't believe that you can increase your level of consciousness simply through the cognitive understanding. What I mean by this is that to truly be at a level and be experiencing yourself as a leader at a certain level of consciousness, you need to have embodied it. You need to feel the level through your bones if you like. It is no use to just think yourself to another level.

That is why I continue to work with leaders to help them gain these fundamental shifts. Each shift may take a few years or more. There is no competition in this, you are where you are and to try and be at a higher level, will in itself probably get in the way of obtaining it!

Models of levels of consciousness

I state in this book that we need to raise levels of consciousness as leaders. But how do we know which level we are in, and how can we move to the next level?

The use of models for levels of consciousness can give us a map of the whole journey we are on. We can then identify where we are right now and more importantly gain support to move to the next level.

There is a general belief that we cannot skip a stage in the model. We must experience being at each stage from birth to death, and some may never reach the higher levels. It is also generally accepted that as you move onto the next level, you incorporate the levels that came before, so you simply gain the flexibility to experience each level.

There are many different models that map an individual's personal development towards higher levels of consciousness. There are also many models that map humanity's conscious development. Each model is coming from the field of learning of the person/group that has developed the model.

So we see models about the development of the psyche that have come from the field of psychology; models about development of the brain function and the brain's capability for neuroplasticity come from neuroscience; models of societal development from anthropology; models of organisational and leadership development from business; models of spiritual development from theology and so forth.

Some of the models so far

One of the oldest models of the development of humanity's consciousness is the Mayan nine-stage model developed in the Mayan culture around 2000BC. This model predicted the key stages of humanity's development from the start of all creation, to the "achievement of godlike status of all-knowing consciousness'" in 2011.

From the West, much of the theory comes from the field of psychology. A key turning point was the development of Humanistic psychology in the mid 20th Century by Maslow and Sutich. Having developed this "whole system" approach to the development of the human psyche, they realized by the late 1970s that they had left out an extremely important element, the spiritual dimension, of the human psyche and developed Transpersonal psychology.

> The renaissance of interest in Eastern spiritual philosophies, various mystical traditions, meditation, ancient and aboriginal wisdom, as well as the widespread psychedelic experimentation during the stormy 1960s made it absolutely clear that a comprehensive and cross-culturally valid psychology had to include observations from such areas as mystical states; cosmic consciousness; psychedelic experiences; trance phenomena; creativity; and religious, artistic, and scientific inspiration.
> - Sutich

Some of these "alternative" models of developing levels of consciousness are the Seven Shamanic levels of consciousness, teaching of Vedante (Hinduism) and the seven levels within the Chakra system (Yoga).

Since the development of Transpersonal psychology and the incorporation of views from around the world, there have been many more developments in the field of models for human consciousness.

Timothy Leary and Robert Anton Wilson proposed the Eight-Circuit Model of Individual Consciousness. Joiner and Josephs have developed a five-stage model of Leadership agility. And Robert Kegan and Lisa Lahey categorize three stages of mind development: the socialized mind, the self-authoring mind and the self-transforming mind.

Richard Barrett's Model for Leadership

I think one of the best sources of information (and inspiration) in this area is Richard Barrett's book *The New Leadership Paradigm*, in which he sets out a comprehensive model for the development of consciousness and what that means for the individual in their life, the leaders within organisations and leaders who lead societies.

Below is his basic model showing our motivation, identity and actions (enabling strategy) at each level of consciousness.

Levels of Consciousness	Motivation	Identity	Enabling Strategy
7. Service	Devoting your life to selfless service in the pursuit of your purpose and your global vision	Self as a member of the human race, living on Earth and embracing full spectrum sustainability	Serving. Fulfilling your destiny by giving back to the world

6. Making a Difference	Actualizing your sense of purpose by collaborating with others to make a difference in the world	Self as a member of a community and/or an affiliation of groups with shared values, purpose and direction	Integrating. Aligning with others who share the same purpose
5. Internal Cohesion	Finding meaning for your life by uncovering your purpose and creating a vision for the future you want to create	Self as a member of a group that shares your values and allows you to connect with your purpose	Self-Actualizing. Aligning fully with who you are
4. Transformation	Embracing your individuality so you can become a fully self-actualized authentic individual	Self as a member of a group that celebrates and encourages your unique abilities and talents	Individuating. Exploring who you are and your talents
3. Self-esteem	Satisfying your need to feel good about yourself and your ability to manage your life and having pride in your performance	Self as a member of or supporter of a group that aligns with your faith, interests, and/or opinions	Differentiating Beginning to separate yourself from others
2. Relationship	Satisfying your need for belonging and feeling loved and accepted by those whom you interact with on a daily basis	Self as member of family or clan with shared heritage	Conforming. Staying safe and loyal to your group
1. Survival	Satisfying your physiological needs and creating a safe, secure environment for self	Self as an individual in a physical body	Surviving. Staying alive

Richard Barrett's seven-stage model of consciousness shows that the first three stages we go through are all about meeting our basic needs, the need to survive, the need to belong and the need for self-worth. He states that our motivations in each of these stages are born out of fear of not having these needs met (as opposed to our motivation in stages 4-7 which is from a place of joy not fear).

Once we have mastered a way in life to meet our ego needs, we will feel safe, have enough money, food, shelter to survive; we feel as if we belong to our particular group of friends and loved ones and we feel good about ourselves. Then we have a chance to transform into level 4 by letting go of the ego all together to recognize the paradox that we are all totally unique and separate, and at the same time, we are all one consciousness.

At any stage in our lives, we can be pulled back into lower levels of consciousness in order to ensure we survive, but we can only see the world through the mindset of the highest level of consciousness we have achieved. So those leaders who have developed to level 3 cannot see the world in the way that those leaders in stage four can. However, those leaders who have reached stage seven can see the world through the perspective of all levels.

He states that the majority of leaders (and people in general) are in stages 1-3. So I have focused much of this book on practical exercises that allow us to move past stages 1 - 3. I end with some examples of basic thought patterns that could be useful to read through to shift to the higher levels of consciousness described in the literature on this topic.

Rooke and Torbert's Model, "Seven Transformations of Leadership'"

This model was developed and tested over 25 years and by interviewing thousands of leaders. Participants were asked to complete 36 sentences that begin with phrases such as "A good leader...," to which responses vary widely:

"... cracks the whip."

"... realizes that it's important to achieve good performance from subordinates."

"... juggles competing forces and takes responsibility for her decisions."

Highly trained evaluators could then paint a picture of how participants interpret their own actions and the world around them; these "pictures" show which one of seven developmental levels.

They also plotted the percentage of participants against each stage to see where the current level of Leadership thinking is.

Action Logic	Characteristic	Strengths	% of Leaders
7. Alchemist	Generates social transformations.	Integrates material, spiritual and societal transformation.	1%
6. Strategist	Generates organizational and personal transformations. Exercises the power of mutual inquiry, vigilance, and vulnerability for both the short and long term.	Effective as a transformational Leader.	4%
5. Individualist	Interweaves competing personal and company action logics. Creates unique structures to resolve gaps between strategy and performance.	Effective in venture and consulting roles.	10%
4. Achiever	Meets strategic goals. Effectively achieves goals through teams; juggles managerial duties and market demands.	Well suited to managerial roles; action and goal orientated	30%

3. Expert	Rules by logic and expertise. Seeks rational efficiency	Good as an individual contributor	38%
2. Diplomat	Avoids overt conflict. Wants to belong; obeys group norms; rarely rocks the boat.	They are good as supportive glue within an office; helps bring people together.	12%
1. Opportunist	Wins any way possible. Self-orientated, manipulative. 'Might is right'	They are good in emergencies and in sales opportunities	5%

They state that "Leaders can move through these categories as their abilities grow, so taking the Leadership Development Profile again several years later can reveal whether a Leader's action logic has evolved."

Spiral Dynamics – model of conscious development for whole societies

Spiral Dynamics is a theory of the development of consciousness within whole societies. The concept was first introduced in the book *Spiral Dynamics* by Don Beck and Chris Cowan in 1996. Although there is some controversy surrounding the current expansion of this model, I feel it is also worth mentioning here.

The book is based on the theory of psychology by Professor Clare W. Graves. The model gives us eight levels of consciousness for whole societies. Each level is represented by a colour and explains how a society at this level will be acting and thinking. This model is explored more in the section below.

An addition to Don Beck and Chris Cowan's model of Spiral Dynamics is the estimation of the percentage of people who are currently operating at each level of consciousness and a percentage of people in power that are operating from each level of consciousness.

Using these estimations we can understand the level of thinking of the majority of Leaders in the world. It is also obvious that if the majority of Leaders were to raise their level of consciousness and be operating at a higher level within the model, business would thrive as it would be there to serve the world and many of the world's current problems could be resolved.

Level (Colour and Label)	Characteristics	Where Seen	Estimated % of world population and % of social power
8. Turquoise Holistic	Universal holistic system, waves of integrated energies, unites feeling with knowledge, multiple levels interwoven into one conscious system. Universal order but in a living, conscious fashion, not based on external rules (level 4) or group bonds (level 6).		0.1% population 1% power

7. Yellow Integrative	Life is a kaleidoscope of natural systems that are interdependent. Flexibility, spontaneity and functionality have the highest priority. Knowledge and competency supersedes power, status or group sensitivity. Good governance over complex world incorporating levels 1-6 thinking.		1% population 5% of power
6. Green The Sensitive Self	The human spirit must be freed from greed, dogma and divisiveness. Feeling and caring supersede cold rationality. Human bonding, ecological sensitivity, networking, cherishing the earth. Anti-hierarchy. Emphasis on dialogue, relationships, multiculturalism, nonlinear thinking.	Ecology, postmodernism, Netherlands idealism, Rogerian counseling, Canadian healthcare, humanistic psychology, World Council of Churches, Greenpeace, ecofeminism, politically correct, human rights	10% of world population (20-25% of American population) 15% power

5. Orange Scientific Achievement	The self 'escapes' from the 'herd mentality' of level 4 and seeks truth and meaning in individualistic terms. Experiential and objective. The world is rational and well-oiled machine with natural laws that can be learned and mastered and manipulated.	Ayn Rand's 'Atlas Shrugged', Wall Street, emerging middle classes around the world, cosmetics industry, trophy hunting, colonialism, the Cold War, fashion industry, materialism, secular humanism	30% population 50% power
4. Blue Mythic Order	Life has meaning, direction and purpose with outcomes defined by all-powerful Other or Order. This righteous Order enforces a code of conduct based on absolutist principal of 'right' and 'wrong'. It controls through punishment and guilt. It rewards the faithful.	Puritan America, Confucian China, Dickensian England, Singapore discipline, totalitarianism, codes of chivalry and honor, religious fundamentalism, Patriotism	40% population 30% power
3. Red Power Gods	First emergence of self distinct from the tribe, powerful, impulsive, egocentric, heroic. Archetypal gods and goddesses. Forces to be reckoned with are good and bad.	The 'terrible twos', rebellious youth, frontier mentalities, feudal kingdoms, gang Leaders, soldiers of fortune, wild rock stars, James Bond villains	20% population 5% power

2. Purple Magical-Animistic	Thinking is magical spirits, good and bad, curses, spells. Forms into ethnic tribes. Spirits exist and bond with the tribe. Kinship and lineage establish political links.	Voodoo beliefs, blood oaths, ancient grudges, good luck charms, family rituals, superstitions, gangs, athletic teams, corporate 'tribes'	10% population 1% power
1. Beige Archaic-Instinctual	Basic survival; food, water, warmth, safety have priority.	First human societies, newborn infants, starving masses	0.1% population 0% power

Chapter Summary

By now you should have a clear understanding of the different levels of consciousness and how they apply to individuals, leaders, organizations as well as whole societies.

You may be able to identify your own level of consciousness, that of other Leaders, your organization and your society (or parts of your society).

CHAPTER 16

The Historical and Global Context For This Book

Introduction

If you've got this far, then you will understand the following:

- What Conscious Leadership is
- How to become a Conscious Leader
- The benefits you will gain for yourself as a Conscious Leader
- The benefits your team and organisation will gain with Conscious Leaders
- The benefits for society as a whole with Conscious Leadership
- The overall journey of conscious development so that you can see what level you may be currently operating from and what the next level looks like

In this chapter, I lay out some of the key historical and global issues that have led me to write this book. I believe that we are in a significant period in history, as one may have felt at the start of the industrial era. We are at the start of the era of waking up to our true reality! We are beginning to understand how we are the creators of our world through our THOUGHTS – hopefully enough people "wake up" and change the way we see ourselves, humanity and the planet.

Serendipity

There is no coincidence that you chose to read this book at this time, in this place. It is perfect timing for you to become a Conscious Leader. It is no coincidence that I have dedicated my career to studying and questioning Leadership and have suddenly understood how to help you become a Conscious Leader.

It is because this is exactly what the world needs right now. We are all in this advancement together! I am just doing my little piece by studying this and writing this book. Much of the rest of the world is moving us in this direction, too, in a multitude of different ways.

My purpose for writing this book was not to help you simply become a better leader so that you can climb the corporate ladder and earn more money – although this is no doubt an indirect result that you will experience if you chose to.

My point is that I have a more pressing need to help you become a Conscious Leader and that is so that you can adapt to the shifts that are happening in this stage of history in the world. Yes, like the old World War II posters said, "Your Country Needs You" – likewise, I say, "The Whole World Needs You." So no pressure!

Globalisation – why you need to have a global perspective

The world is rapidly becoming truly global. Boundaries between countries are more permeable. Trade of goods, migration of people and communication are just a few of the things that are flowing across countries with fewer barriers.

It's easier to travel, to use a credit card across many currencies and to find the homogenous corporate faces of McDonalds and HSBC Bank, etc. in more far-flung places in the world.

Many of you as leaders are expected to take a more global mindset and to understand far higher levels of complexity when taking decisions. Because the world is now so interconnected, to reach an end goal, a leader may need to facilitate many different points of view and differing motivations. To move forward, they still need to truly gain buy-in from disparate groups of people. Their role is less command and control of people. It is more inspiring and helping people raise their levels of consciousness and agree upon a course of action that benefits the whole and not just their own group.

Understanding that we are all connected, not separate

The concept of a universal consciousness is based on the belief that everything is connected and that if conscious thought and memories are a real thing that just can't be seen and touched (like electricity), then all of consciousness, today and in the whole history of human consciousness, can be accessed if we know how. This ability to disconnect from our everyday way of seeing our individual dramas and connecting to a larger, more profound source of universal consciousness is the skill that leaders now need in order to help others do the same and begin to make decisions for the good of the whole rather than for the good of the powerful at the expense of the less powerful.

In the West, leaders have (like all of us) been conditioned by a society that fundamentally focuses on separateness and therefore competition for resources. The fundamental belief in the West during the 19th and 20th centuries was one of superiority over the rest of the world. Other parts of the world were viewed as uncivilized, and therefore, any beliefs those cultures held were either unknown or dismissed.

The separateness did not just extend to West and East, but to individual countries, and within those countries, individual areas. Within one society, you had clear separation between the classes (particularly in England) and separation (by law in the US) based on skin colour. The roles of men and women and their capabilities were also kept very separate.

With all these separations, one side held the power and the other was subordinated.

This meant that the world was only utilizing a very small percentage of the human resources available to it. It also meant that those resources that did fit the criteria for employment, and leadership tended to think the same way, weakening the humankind's ability to innovate and adapt to change. This inequality also leads to the less powerful people retaliating to try and gain equality. If those in power do not hear the complaints of the less powerful and move towards making society equal, then eventually, the less powerful often resort to violence against the powerful.

We are beginning to understand that we are all co-creating the cultures we work in, the negative or positive energy fields in our homes, in our communities and ultimately across the globe. We can no longer point the finger and blame "the other." Leaders at higher levels of consciousness understand that the whole system is one and each part in that system (each person, each organisation, each country) is inter-connected.

Making business work for society not the other way round

The culture that emerged through the general leadership of the day reflected the beliefs about the world and level of consciousness of the majority of Leaders. Leaders of profit generating organisations have had to focus on generating profit and sometimes this has been at the expense of their customers, workers, or others affected by the actions of this organisation.

> Our business leaders must stop seeking to be the best in the world and start seeking to be the best for the world
> -Richard Barrett

Advanced business leaders are now realizing that if they focus on doing the best thing for their customers/clients and staff, the actions of their organisation cannot fail to increase profits because so long as the organisation is charging properly for the value it is adding to its customers lives, then the natural laws of economics will apply, and the value will be repaid with money.

Why we can't keep producing the same type of leaders – be the Leadership model for the future

We are coming to the end of the Industrial Age in the West. We are no longer the major makers of physical products, but rather the thinkers behind them. We have our intellectual property to sell to those who are going through their own industrial revolution.

Our value to the world is in knowledge of and experience in building and leading organisation through our own Industrial Age. We can help others do the same without making the mistakes we have already made. We are also still the major consumers for the world.

What does this really mean for you as leaders, though?

The type of leaders we needed during the Industrial Age were strong, command and control style leaders whose business goals were to make more products in less time with less cost. The world did not expect them to think of the negative ramifications on the environment or the exploitation of people to get these business results. Nearly all of the Industrial Age leaders were male, and society had very different expectations of them and therefore very different levels of tolerance to how they led.

In the new world, you are required to treat everyone equally and to use the strength of diversity to lead your organisations. Strong, command and control style management is often not respected because with the rise of the individual rights and the breakdown of the class system, each person in an organisation expects to be respected as an equal contributor.

In Seth Goddin's book *The Icarus Deception*, he states "The industrial model of command and control and the avoidance of failure now permeates every corner of the culture." He suggests that we are now heading into a "connection economy," which involves a complex swap of information, expectations and culture. He urges readers to wake up to the brainwashing that has occurred to them as they grew up in our culture and to have the courage to create their 'true art." By this he means: do not blindly conform, but listen to your own heart's desire and bring whatever it wants you to contribute in your lifetime into the world.

Organisations with leaders operating from a Western, Industrial Age level of consciousness will fall behind. The world is changing so to keep leading in the same old way will inevitably fail.

This book explains why those of you who invest the energy and who have the courage to develop your levels of consciousness will be the ones who will automatically rise to top leadership positions and will be mentally equipped to bring success to their organisations.

How social responsibility will lead to your downfall or to lower costs for borrowing!

People are much more educated about what organisations have done to bring their products to market. So you are called upon to have a much wider perspective and in some cases to consider the effects of your decisions globally. Consumers are less likely to allow organisations to get away with exploitation or damage to the environment in order to increase their profits.

We are all aware of many brands that have been highlighted and then boycotted because consumers in the West were angry about the exploitation of local, often developing world, workers.

Nike is a good example of a brand that could have been damaged due to the exploitation of its workers becoming widely known. However, the leaders addressed consumers' concerns and rescued the brand through being seen to change the way they operated.

Mark Ritson in his article *'Social Responsibility: The Nike Story'* states that:

> 2005 saw the publication of Nike's second Corporate Responsibility Report. It stands as a remarkable document because for the first time a global clothing brand revealed all of its production locations, the status of labour policies in those locations and the systematic manner in which it intended to improve its suppliers' employment practices.

Nike continues to aim to be transparent and caring in its approach to Corporate Social Responsibility (CSR).

Recently, it has been found that Leaders who actively champion CSR are creating a financial advantage for their organisations when it comes to the cost of capital. The winners of the 2011 Moskowitz Prize (an annual prize for best research on CSR), Sadok El Ghoula, Omrane Guedhamib, Chuck C. Y. Kwokb and Dev R. Mishrac wrote an article entitled 'Does Corporate Social Responsibility Affect the Cost of Capital?' Below is an extract:

> We examine the effect of corporate social responsibility (CSR) on the cost of equity capital for a large sample of U.S. firms. Using several approaches to estimate firms' ex ante cost of equity, we find that firms with better CSR scores exhibit cheaper equity financing. In particular, our findings suggest that investment in improving responsible employee relations, environmental policies, and product strategies contributes substantially to reducing firms' cost of equity.

Why Walking Your Talk Is Vital – There is Nowhere to Hide!

Due to the world wide web, consumers can spread information about what actions organisations are taking in the real world and how this often does not align with their stated values.

The Wall Street Journal in 2010 published the following statistics: 92% of online consumers have more confidence in information found online than anything given to them by a sales person representing a company.

Leaders are called upon to be honest and stop trying to cover up their mistakes. Otherwise they bring reputational damage to themselves and the organisations they lead.

In 2010, Nestlé had a 90,000 online fan base. Greenpeace, in campaigning against deforestation, named Nestle's "unsustainable palm oil policy" as a major cause. In response to that, many online fans posted angry comments on Nestlé's facebook page. Nestlé's lack of honesty and the decision to take down the angry, negative comments from the Facebook page and posting their own defensive position, led to a PR and branding disaster.

How to attract the future top talent – what they want

Generation Y grew up in a world where mobile phones, Facebook, easy air travel and global warming already existed. Due to the social and environmental condition of the world that they have been raised in, they hold particular world views and values.

In 2012, 90% of MBA students at Stanford Graduate School of Business ranked "socially good" as more important to them than "salary" when choosing a potential employer. This is not only hopeful for the world at large, but also means that those leaders who also value social good and steer their companies in this direction will attract the next generation of talent.

Developments in the field of leadership

The academic field of excellence in leadership is full of models that each seem to be saying the same basic thing. That is, the higher level of consciousness a person reaches, the more successful they will be as leaders. So it seems that the fields of study in human consciousness and the field of business leadership are merging.

David Rooke and William R. Torbert, in their book *Seven Transformations of Leadership* state;

> Most developmental psychologists agree that what differentiates Leaders is not so much their philosophy of Leadership, their personality, or their style of management. Rather, it's their internal "action logic" – how they interpret their surroundings and react when their power or safety is challenged. Relatively few Leaders, however, try to understand their own action logic, and fewer still have explored the possibility of changing it.

Rooke and Torbert go on to explain each level of Leadership and how you are being as a leader at each of the seven levels.

This is very exciting for me because for years, I have intuitively been working with leaders to develop themselves personally to develop their emotional maturity and their connection to energetic fields and universal consciousness. I may not have actually stated that this is what I was doing, for fear that I would have no clients! However, it feels as if there have been enough developments from reputable academics that are held in high esteem by the business world for me to be more explicit about my work.

I recently had some spare time in London whilst waiting to meet friends for dinner. I was near Waterston's bookshop in Trafalgar Square and having a love of books and bookshops, I decided to go in for a browse.

I initially went to the section for Business and Leadership, and I noticed a middle-aged man in a business suit looking through some of these books. He looked slightly surprised to see me pick up a heavy weight book on leadership as I was dressed for dinner in town – not exactly looking like a corporate type! I smiled at his expression and said, "I study leadership, but don't worry I'll be popping over to the mind, body, spirit section in a minute too." He smiled and replied, "Oh, I don't go in for all this New Age, hippy spiritual stuff myself. I need to have concrete evidence for things."

I totally understand his view, and it got me thinking that perhaps the field of business leadership had traditionally been about concrete evidence based information. However, it seems to me that the knowledge and wisdom from the mind, body, spirit section is slowly being incorporated into works on leadership.

Traditionally, leadership and management books in the business section have focused on how the leader can influence the external world directly – i.e., what they should "do" in the external world (or what they should 'do' to the external world).

Body, mind, and spirit books are more focused on how the reader can influence their internal world in order to then have an effect in the external world, or to change their experience and understanding of the external world.

Academics in the field of leadership have been asking, "Is it possible to train someone to become a good Leader?" and "What is that rare quality that a good leader has, so that we can take it and train others to have it?"

Those developing the field of body, mind, and spirit have been asking, "How do we achieve a happy, healthy life? How do we have good relationships with others and what is the purpose of our lives, how can we contribute to the world?" In this book, I aim to show that the most successful leaders in the future will be those who practice the art of a happy, healthy life. They will then have good relationships with others, understand their purpose and know how to make their contribution to the world.

So the field of leadership development is expanding to focus on "who" a leader is because we now understand that **what a Leader does** is predicated on **what they think** about their world. We are beginning to realize that if we could measure and improve what a leader thinks about themselves, about others and about their world, we can help develop them at a fundamental level. We would no longer have to train leaders with a "one size fits all" method of running organisations. We would have helped that leader recode their own thought processes. They will be operating from an entirely "upgraded system" and therefore be able to cope with more complexity, more uncertainty, greater innovation and be better adapted to the demands of creating successful societies and organisations in the 21st century.

In the past, the "who" someone was often got attributed to which school they went to and who their family was. In knowing their background, we could assume they had certain values and beliefs that were in accordance with the western business culture of the day. To some extent, this still exists in the UK. However, as more of the population gains access to leadership opportunities, there has been a need to independently test who a person is despite the circumstances of their birth and upbringing. The rise of personality profiling tools has gone some way to identifying what a person thinks about certain things, but does not really test a person's level of consciousness.

In the West right now, there is a fundamental shift in beliefs about how we should govern and do business in the world. We are drawing on beliefs and ways of being from across the world and trying to incorporate wisdom from belief systems such as Buddhism, American Indian culture and Yoga, to name a few. The beliefs that have underpinned the way leaders have led their countries and organisations for the last century or so, is being more and more challenged by new thinkers. Leadership as a topic sits within a larger framework of discussions around sustainable global economics, environmental protection for future generations and social justice.

Chapter Summary

This chapter discusses:

- Some of the key developments that are happening in our world today and why this has led to a "waking up" for many people.
- Why this is the time to become a Conscious Leader

Acknowledgements

A big thank you to Richard Barrett, Goran Tomson, Philip Mix, Robin Field-Smith, Dee Clayton, Silke Elvery, Joe Chambers, Tony Kypreos and Jodie Moore for all their honest and valuable feedback on various drafts of this book.

Wayne Oliver at wayne@bitecreative.co.uk for his illustrations.

My family and friends for giving me the emotional support needed to keep running my business to pay the mortgage, as well as helping me take the time out to write this book during a particularly challenging period in my life. Thank you.

Don't Just Put This Book On The Shelf! – Take Action

Reading theoretical books on leadership – even ones like this that have practical exercises for you to do – is unlikely to lead to you fast tracking your development to a higher level of consciousness.

The reason for this is that you are using your own thinking to try and develop. It is much easier and quicker to have a professional observer to your own way of being who is trained to understand how your thoughts are creating your problems and challenges to work with you.

If you have enjoyed this book and would like to explore more of these concepts, please contact us for more information about the courses and 1:1 coaching programmes that we run to help you IMPLEMENT these concepts and become the best leader and model of leadership you can be.

Leadership Programme – includes 1:1 private coaching conducted by Rebecca Watson worldwide via Skype or face-to-face in London, UK plus four quarterly workshops where you get to meet and work with the other leaders in this programme.

Leadership Retreats – which currently run each year in Spain in October.

Team Coaching and Board Facilitation – to support the Leaders of Organisations to create the results they want to see in the world.

Speaking Engagements and Bespoke Workshops – Rebecca is available to speak on this topic and expand on particular areas of interest to your group

www.bromptonassociates.com

Yoga and Coaching Holidays
Rebecca has also set up a separate business to allow you to work with her privately at an affordable price if your organization will not sponsor your coaching.

www.clearmindyogaretreats.com

Bibliography

Barrett, Richard. <u>The New Leadership Paradigm,</u> self-published 2010.

Borg, James. <u>Body Language: 7 Easy Lessons to Master the Silent Language</u>, Harlow, England: Pearson Education, 2008.

Brazier, David. <u>Zen Therapy</u>, London, England: Constable and Company, 1996.

Campbell, Joseph. <u>The Hero With A Thousand Faces</u>, New York City, USA: Pantheon Books, 1949.

Carlyle, Marie-Claire. How to <u>Become A Money Magnet,</u> London, England: Hay House, 2009.

Charvet, Shelle Rose. <u>Words That Change Minds: Mastering the Language of Influence</u>, Iowa, USA: Kendall Hunt Publishing, 1997.

Christensen, John; Paul, Harry; Lundin, Stephen C. <u>Fish! for Life: A Remarkable Way to Achieve Your Dreams,</u> New York, USA: Hyperion Books, 2004.

Collins, Jim. <u>Good to Great</u>, London, England: Random House Business Books, 2001.

Cook-Grueter, Susanne R. <u>Mature Ego Development: A Gateway to Ego Transcendence, Journal of Adult Development, Vol 7, No. 4</u>. 2008.

Covey, Stephen. <u>Seven Habits of Highly Successful People</u>, London, England: Simon & Schuster, 2004.

Covey, Stephen. <u>The 8th Habit: From Effectiveness to Greatness</u>, London, England: Simon and Schuster, 2006.

Cutler, Howard C. and His Holiness the Dalai Lama. <u>The Art of Happiness</u>, London, England: Hodder & Stoughton, 2009.

Doherty, Nora and Guyler, Marcelas. <u>Guide to Workplace Mediation & Conflict Resolution: Rebuilding Working Relationships</u>, London, England: Kogan Page limited, 2008.

Evans, Julie. <u>Philosophy for Life and Other Dangerous Situations</u>, London, England: Rider, 2013.

Farhi, Donna. Bringing Yoga to Life: The Everyday Practice of

Enlightened Living. New York, USA: Harper Collins, 2004.
Gladwell, Malcolm. <u>Outliers</u>, London, England: Allen Lane, 2008.

Godin, Seth. <u>The Icarus Deception: How high will you fly?</u> London, England: Penguin Books, 2012.

Goleman, Daniel. <u>Emotional Intelligence: Why it Can Matter More Than IQ</u>, London, England: Bloomsbury Publishing, 1996.

Goleman, Daniel. <u>Social Intelligence: The New Science of Human Relationships</u>, London, England: Arrow Books, 2007.

Heath, Chip & Dan. <u>Switch: How to change things when change is hard</u>, London, England: Random House Business Books, 2010.

Hendrix, Harville. <u>Getting the Love you Want: A Guide for Couples</u>, London, England: Simon and Schuster, 2005.

Hill, Napolean. <u>Think and Grow Rich The Original Classic</u>, Chichester, England: Capstone Publishing, 2009.

Jeffers, Susan. <u>Feel The Fear And Do It Anyway</u>, London, England: Ebury Press, 2007.

Kegan, Robert and Lahay, Lisa.<u>Immunity to Change: How to Overcome It and Unlock the Potential in Yourself and Your Organization (Leadership for the Common Good)</u>, Boston, USA: Harvard Business

School Publishing.

Leary-Joyce, Judith. <u>The Psychology of Success: Secrets of serial achievement</u>, London, England: Pearson Prentice Hall, 2009.

Malan, David H. <u>Individual Psychotherapy and the Science of Psychodynamics</u>, London, England: Arnold Publishers, 2001.

Maurer, Dr Robert. <u>One Small Step Can Change Your Life</u>, New York, USA: Workman Publishing Company, 2004.

Moorjani, Anita. <u>Dying to be Me</u>, London, England: Hay House, 2012.

Obama, Barack. <u>Dreams From My Father</u>, Edinburgh, fScotland: Canongate Books, 2007.

Renshaw Ben. <u>Successful but Something Missing</u>, London, England: Rider 2000.

Robbins, Antony. <u>Notes From A Friend</u>, London, England: Simon and Schuster, 1996.

Rooke, David and Torbert, William R. <u>Seven Transformations of Leaders</u>. Boston, USA: Harvard Business Review, April 2005.

Ronson, Jon. <u>The Psychopath Test: A Journey Through the Madness Industry</u>. London, England: Picador, 2011

Sadok El Ghoula, Omrane Guedhamib, Chuck C. Y. Kwokb and Dev R. Mishrac. Article: 'Does corporate social responsibility affect the cost of capital?' Journal of Banking & Finance, Volume 35, Issue 9, September 2011, Pages 2388-2406.

Sharma, Robin. <u>The Monk Who Sold His Ferrari</u>, London, England: Harper Element, 2007.

Thornton, Christine. <u>Group and Team Coaching: The Essential Guide (Essential Coaching Skills and Knowledge)</u>, Hove, England: Routledge, 2010.

Unger, Craig, <u>The Fall of the House of Bush</u>, London, England: Simon and Schuster, 2007.

Wallace, Danny. <u>Yes Man,</u> London, England: Ebury Press, 2005.

Walsh, Neale Donald. <u>Conversations With God, Book 1: An Uncommon Dialogue,</u> London, England: Hodder and Stoughton, 1997.

Whitmore, Sir John. <u>Coaching for Performance,</u> London, England: Nicholas Brealey Publishing, 1992.

Wilber, Ken. <u>A Theory of Everything: An Integral Vision for Business, Politics, Science and Spirituality.</u> Dublin, Ireland: Gateway, 2001.